Fred B Mason

Gibbs' Illustrated Handbook to St. Albans

containing a sketch of its history, and a description of its abbey, its antiquities, and other objects of interest. Third Edition

Fred B Mason

Gibbs' Illustrated Handbook to St. Albans
containing a sketch of its history, and a description of its abbey, its antiquities, and other objects of interest. Third Edition

ISBN/EAN: 9783337095888

Printed in Europe, USA, Canada, Australia, Japan

Cover: Foto ©Andreas Hilbeck / pixelio.de

More available books at **www.hansebooks.com**

Gibbs' Illustrated
HANDBOOK TO ST. ALBANS

CONTAINING

A Sketch of its History, and a Description of its Abbey, its Antiquities, and other Objects of Interest.

BY

FRED. B. MASON.

THIRD EDITION.

ST. ALBANS:
PRINTED AND PUBLISHED BY GIBBS AND BAMFORTH,
"HERTS ADVERTISER OFFICE."

1884.

PREFACE TO THIRD EDITION.

In the Preface to the Second Edition of this Handbook, published in October, 1876, I alluded to the fact that the work of restoring St. Albans Abbey was then languishing for want of funds. A few months afterwards, an event of the first importance in the history of St. Albans, stimulated it afresh. The new See of St. Albans was formed, the Abbey was raised to the dignity of a Cathedral Church, the first Bishop of St. Albans was enthroned within its venerable walls, and the ancient town became a city. The restoration of the Abbey was continued with renewed vigour, and made substantial progress. The great architect to whom it had been entrusted was not, however, to witness the completion of the work in which he took so enthusiastic and loving an interest. After the death of Sir Gilbert Scott, in March, 1878, a proposal to construct a roof of the original high pitch over the Nave was, after a rather heated controversy, resolved upon and carried out. This was followed by another great structural alteration made in the face of strong opposition—the rebuilding by Sir Edmund Beckett of the west front of the Abbey at his own cost and in accordance with his own designs. Through Sir Edmund's munificence, the restoration of the south side of the Nave, which was carried to a certain point by Sir Gilbert Scott, is again being proceeded with. Money, however, is still wanted to complete the restoration of the Lady and Ante-Chapels.

The present Edition of the Handbook has been carefully revised, and the information it contains brought down to the present time, I trust it may not prove less acceptable than the preceding Editions. The portion which forms a Guide to the Abbey has again been kept distinct from the rest of the work, to facilitate its publication in a separate form for the use of visitors, and I have endeavoured to make it as complete as the limits of the space assigned to it will permit. I have to make especial acknowledgment of the kind and ready help I have received, from Mr. John Chapple, who has materially lessened for me the difficulty of preparing, while living at a distance from St. Albans, a new Edition for the Press.

F. B. M.

OSWESTRY,
  December, 1883.

CONTENTS.

CHAPTER I.

The City of Verulam—Its situation—Its importance and magnitude—The seat of a British prince—Attacked by Julius Cæsar—Made a Municipium—Its inhabitants slaughtered by Queen Boadicea—The wealth of the City—Attacked by the Romans—Rebuilt—Its remains—The Roman Wall—The size of the City—Roman coins, &c.—St. Alban—His martyrdom—His miracles—The spread of Christianity—The erection of a Church on the site of his martyrdom—Death of Amphibalus—St. German's Chapel—The City of Verulam destroyed by the Saxons 7

CHAPTER II.

King Offa—His resolve to found a Monastery—His search for the relics of the martyr—The miraculous light—The finding of the body of St. Alban—Its removal to a shrine—Offa's journey to Rome—The foundation of the Monastery—The death of Offa and of Willegod, the first abbot—The growth of the Monastery—Vulsig and Vulnoth—The Shrine of St. Alban despoiled—Ulsinus, the founder of the town of St. Albans—Aelfric purchases the King's Fishpool—Ealdred and Eadmer—Excavations at Verulam—Discovery of a History of St. Alban—Leofric and Aelfric the Second—Destruction of the Royal Palace—Leofstan—Watling Street protected from thieves and wild beasts—Abbot Frederick and his opposition to William the Conqueror—Paul, the first Norman Abbot—Rebuilds the Abbey Church—His austerity—D'Albini, fifteenth abbot—Consecration of the Abbey Church—Geoffrey de Gorham—His love of splendour—Founds the Nunnery of Sopwell—Origin of the Liberty of St. Alban 14

CHAPTER III.

Robert de Gorham, eighteenth abbot—Obtains privileges and immunities for the Monastery from Pope Adrian—Gorhambury—Abbot Symon—Warren de Cambridge, twentieth abbot—Abbot John de Cella—Rebuilds the west end of the Church—William de Trumpington, twenty-second abbot—Finishes the west end of the Church—King John and the Barons—Abbot John, of Hertford—Royal visits—Matthew Paris—Roger de Norton, twenty-fourth abbot—Dispute between the abbot and the townspeople—The Constable of Hertford is beheaded—Queen Eleanor's Cross—Hugh de Eversden, twenty-seventh abbot—His contentions with the townspeople—Erects the Lady Chapel—Abbot Wallingford—His successful defence of ecclesiastical domination—Michael de Mentmore, twenty-ninth abbot—A Royal Baptism—The King of France brought to St. Albans—Wat's Tyler's Insurrection—The abbot beautifies the Church and rebuilds the great gate—John of Wheathamstead, thirty-third abbot—Repairs the Abbey fabric—Humphrey, Duke of Gloucester—The abbot evades the Mortmain Act—Abbot Stoke—Burial of Duke Humphrey—Re-election of Abbot Wheathamstead . . 22

CHAPTER IV.

The Wars of the Roses—The first battle of St. Albans—Defeat of the King's army—The abbot counsels moderation—The second battle of St. Albans—Defeat of the Yorkists—Re-union of the king and queen—Plunder of the town—The Earl of March proclaimed king—A royal charter—William Wallingford, thirty-sixth abbot—Erects the altar screen—Introduction of the Art of Printing—Abbot Ramryge—Cardinal Wolsey—The beginning of the end—A commission appointed by the King—Richard Boreman, fortieth and last abbot—His surrender of the Abbey—Dissolution of the Monastery. 29

CHAPTER V.

The Borough of St. Albans—Domesday Book—Charters of Richard I. and Edward VI.—Successive Charters granted by Mary and Elizabeth—The Grammar School and Wine Licenses—Charters of James I., Charles I., Charles II. and James II.—The latter declared void—The Municipal Reform Act 35

CONTENTS.

CHAPTER VI.

St. Albans in Olden Time—The Martyrdom of Tankerfield—The High Sheriff of Herts, with his retinue, taken prisoners by Oliver Cromwell—Town improvements—Disfranchisement of St. Albans 38

CHAPTER VII.

Modern town of St. Albans—View of it from the Verulam Hills—The situation of the Town, its topography, trade, and population—The Liberty of St. Albans—The Bishopric of St. Albans. 42

CHAPTER VIII.

St. Michael's Church—Its restoration—The Tomb of Francis Bacon—Its inscription—Gorhambury—Becomes the property of Sir Nicholas Bacon about the year 1550—He builds a new house—Queen Elizabeth's visits to Gorhambury—Lord Verulam retires to Gorhambury after his disgrace—The Grimston Family—Gorhambury House—Sopwell Nunnery—Its origin and history—The Holywell—St. Stephen's Church—The curious Brass Eagle—The Clock Tower—Traditions as to its origin—The date of the Tower—The Curfew Bell—Restoration of the Tower—The Corn Exchange—The Town Hall—St. Peter's Church—Its origin—Date of the present building—Repairs and alterations—Interior of the Church—Singular inscription—Monuments of interest 46

CHAPTER IX.

St. Albans clergymen ejected by the Act of Uniformity—Pemberton's Almshouses—Tradition as to their origin—Lord Chief Justice Pemberton—The Marlborough Buildings—Christ Church—The Dissenting Chapels—The New Gaol 56

CHAPTER X.

The Abbey Church—Its restoration— The Abbey as seen in the distance—Its associations—Its form and material—The Central Tower and Turrets—Remains of the Cloisters—The Lady Chapel—The Western Entrance—Interior of the Abbey from the Western Entrance—The Nave—Its varying styles of Architecture—Examples of Early English and Decorated Styles in Contrast—Mouldings of the Arches—Reconstruction of the Nave—The work of John de Cella and of William de Trumpington—Destruction of Norman Piers—Decorated work of Hugh de Eversden—The Great West Window—Ancient Piscina—Discovery of Stone Coffins—The Roof—Sir John Mandeville—Alexander Neckham—Series of Frescoes on the Norman Piers—The Chapel of St. Andrew—The Forensic Parlour—St. Cuthbert's or the Rood Screen—Dedication of the Altars—The Organ 63

CHAPTER XI.

The Choir—The Font—The Choir Ceiling—Discovery of the Original Paintings—South Aisle of Baptistery—Memorial Windows—Tomb and Piscina—Roger and Sigar—The Abbots' Door—Apsidal Chapels—The Slype—The Tower—Saxon Columns—The Presbytery—The Wallingford Screen—The Altar-steps and Pavement—Restorations—Tomb of Abbot Ramryge—Tomb of Abbot Wheathamstead—Monumental Brasses and Inscriptions—The New Pulpit—North Aisle of Presbytery—North Transept—The Transept Windows—Ascent to the Tower—The Belfry 78

CHAPTER XII.

South Aisle of the Presbytery—Discovery of Perpendicular Doorway and Screen—Altar-Table—Memorial Window—Monumental Inscriptions—Altar-Tomb—Tomb of Humphrey, Duke of Gloucester—Inscription to his Memory—Saint's Chapel—Remains of Duke Humphrey—Discovery of the Shrine of St. Alban—Watcher's Gallery—Discovery of an Altar—Ante-Chapel and Shrine of St. Amphibalus—Lady Chapel—Sir Gilbert Scott's Report—Completion of the Lady Chapel by Abbot Eversden—Its Windows, &c.—Curious Passage—Abbot Norton—Restorations—List of Abbots of St. Albans 89

HANDBOOK TO ST. ALBANS.

CHAPTER I.

The City of Verulam—Its situation—Its importance and magnitude—The seat of a British prince—Attacked by Julius Cæsar—Made a Municipium—Its inhabitants slaughtered by Queen Boadicea—The wealth of the City—Attacked by the Romans—Rebuilt—Its remains—The Roman Wall—The size of the City—Roman coins, &c.—St. Alban—His martyrdom—His miracles—The spread of Christianity—The erection of a Church on the site of his martyrdom—Death of Amphibalus—St. German's Chapel—The City of Verulam destroyed by the Saxons.

THE famous City of Verulam, of which St. Alban's is the modern representative, and the memorials of whose ancient greatness exist to this day, was situate on the side of what are now called the Verulam Hills, at the foot of which runs the little river Ver. The history of Verulam, or Verulamium, the village on the Ver, is for the most part obscured by the mist of antiquity. That it was once a place of very considerable importance is not only recorded in history, but is verified by the vestiges of its departed glory. Even if history were altogether silent on the subject, we should have in the ruins extant sufficient evidence of its having been " no mean city." But when we call history to our aid we find that Verulam was a great city at the time of the Roman invasion of Britain by Julius Cæsar, and in all probability the place where one of the chief of the British princes, Cassivellaunus, resided and held his court. It is believed, on weighty grounds, to be the city which Cæsar described in his Commentaries as being defended by woods and marshes:—*Silvis paludibusque munitum.* Part of the woods still remains, and the pool of water called "Fishpool," which covered the meadows bounding its walls on the north-east side, gave its name to one of the streets of St. Alban's, which to this day is known by that designation. Cæsar attacked the city, and neither the strength of its natural fortifications nor the valour of its defenders could save it from falling into his hands. The inhabitants of Verulam afterwards became reconciled to their conquerors, and as a reward for their friendly conduct, and for the military services they rendered to the Roman arms, Verulam was endowed with the honours and privileges of a *Municipium*, or Free City. It held this high rank (which very few cities possessed *) as early as the time of the Emperor Nero. But the devotion of its inhabitants to the Roman power afterwards drew down on them the vengeance of the indignant British Queen, Boadicea, who (A.D. 61), after the destruction of Camelodunum and Londinum, attacked the Roman colony of Verulam, and massacred its inhabitants. Tacitus records that seventy thousand persons fell at Verulam, London, and other less important places, by the hands of the Britons, under the command of the Soldier-Queen of the Iceni. The wealth of the city, as well as its large population, formed an inducement to the Britons to attack it; and Tacitus insinuates that they passed other places without assault for the sake of the plunder to be acquired here. The Britons were in their turn defeated by the Roman general, Suetonius Paulinus, who slaughtered the inhabitants of Verulam. The city was afterwards rebuilt, and the Britons remained in quiet submission to the authority of the Roman Government. Verulam regained its former greatness. But little more, however, is really known of its history.

The vestiges of the departed greatness of the city are sufficient to give us some idea of its proportions and extent. Camden says, "The situation of this place is well known to have been close by the town of St. Albans . . . . nor hath it yet lost its ancient name, for it is still commonly

---

* York and Verulam were the only *municipia* in Great Britain ; that is, the only cities whose inhabitants possessed the rights of Roman citizens. The names of the other chief Roman colonies existing at this early period were Richborough, London, Colchester, Bath, Caerleon, Gloucester, Lincoln, and Chester.

called Verulam; although nothing of that remains beside ruins of walls, chequered pavements, and Roman coins, which they now and then dig up." * Fragments of the Roman wall which once surrounded the city still serve to mark the great extent of its area; and it has been said that the sites of various streets may even now be traced out by the growth and colour of the vegetation upon the surface. The course of the principal street ran from south-east to north-west. The masses of Roman wall which remain show clearly the strength and excellence of Roman masonry. The wall surrounding the city was about twelve feet in thickness; it was composed of layers of flints embedded in a strong cement of lime, small gravel, and coarse sand, and interspersed with rows of large Roman tiles. † One of the entrances to the city appears to have been near the massive fragment of the wall called "Gorham's block." The banks and ditches on the south and west sides are in the best state of preservation. Extensive discoveries of Roman remains have been made from time to time, and many of these remains have been deposited in our principal museums. The great antiquary, Camden, whom we have before quoted, writes: "Were I to relate what common report affirms of the many Roman coins, statues of gold and silver, vessels, marble pillars, cornices, and wonderful monuments of ancient art dug up here, I should scarcely be believed."

Many curious discoveries have been made in modern times. In 1719 an urn, twelve small lachrymatories, a

* The late Dr. Black, F.S.A., a very learned but somewhat eccentric antiquary, was of opinion that the whole of Verulam, or Verulam proper, was not confined to the south side of the river. He expended a considerable amount of ingenuity in support of the theory that what is regarded as the site of the ancient city is really the site of a large fortified camp or military town, and that it was not the Verulam of Tacitus, of Antoninus, and of Ptolemy. The municipal city, he contended, was mainly on the other side of the water; in fact, that the present town of St. Albans is identical with the ancient *Municipium* mentioned by Tacitus, as having been destroyed by Boadicea. It is certain, however, that the town on the south side of the river was entirely surrounded by a fortified wall. Dr. Black's theory has been received with little if any favour by other antiquaries.

† Measuring about sixteen inches by thirteen; they are bound together so adhesively that it is very difficult to take one away from the wall without breaking it.

large long jar, several smaller vessels, coins, pateræ, &c., were dug up, with various other Roman remains, at a little distance from the city walls near the river Ver. A great number of Roman coins and remains have been since disinterred, and many of them are in the possession of inhabitants of the town.*

In August, 1869, when the British Archæological Association held its congress at St. Albans, some excavations were very skilfully carried out on the site of ancient Verulam, by means of which the course of the principal streets (running north-east and south-west) was distinctly traced, and the exact width of the roads ascertained. One of these streets formed part of the great military road from London to the north-west. The city itself formed an oval, about three-quarters of a mile long by half a mile wide. The foundations and tesseræ of Roman villas were also laid bare. The remains of an ancient Roman theatre—the only Roman theatre, it is said, yet found in this country—had been previously discovered by the late Mr. Grove Lowe, the stage, proscenium, and orchestra of which were clearly discernible. In a paper read before the Congress, Mr. J. W. Grover pointed out a close resemblance between the theatre discovered at Pompeii and that of Verulam, and also a general resemblance between the two cities. In St. Michael's Churchyard, which was almost the centre of ancient Verulam, some massive Roman foundations were discovered, and Mr. Grover conjectures that this was the site of the ancient temple of the city, which was probaly dedicated to Apollo, as the worship of St. Michael in Christian times succeeded the worship of that heathen deity.

We now have to speak of the event which more than any other is associated with the ancient city of Verulam, the event to which that city owes its chief celebrity, and the less ancient town of St. Albans its name and origin.

---

* Some interesting Roman sepulchral urns and other remains were discovered in St. Stephen's Churchyard in 1848, and were taken care of by the late vicar, the Rev. M. R. Southwell. A very beautiful glass bottle of Roman work, found in St. Michael's Churchyard, is in the possession of the Earl of Verulam. Some of the coins which have been found were struck at Verulam by Tasciovanus, a British prince, who made that city his chief capital.

The martyrdom of Albanus, or Alban, has been so much the subject of monkish fable—the miraculous legends born of superstition, that it is impossible to determine where the truth lies. The marvellous incidents said to have attended the execution of "the proto-martyr of Britain" are such as may well stagger the belief of the most credulous, although the historian Collier appears to have no misgivings as to their reality.

Albanus was, we are told, an eminent Roman citizen who lived at Verulam towards the end of the third century. In his youth he took a journey to Rome, and was for seven years a soldier of the Emperor Dioclesian, under whose persecution he afterwards suffered martyrdom. On his return to Verulam he came a convert to the Christian religion, and sheltered a deacon of the Church with whom he had journeyed to Rome, and who had fled from Wales to Verulam, to avoid the dreadful persecution which had been instituted by the Emperor Dioclesian against the Christians. This man's name was Amphibalus, and he is supposed to have been the instrument of Alban's conversion. The retreat of Amphibalus was unfortunately discovered, and the judge of the city sent some soldiers to arrest him. But Albanus, having received warning of their approach and intended purpose, in an heroic spirit of self-sacrifice, disguised himself in the habit of his guest, whom he had privately sent away, and generously offered himself to the soldiers as the man for whom they were in search. He was bound and taken before the judge, when he threw off his cloak and declared himself a Christian. The judge insisted on his offering a sacrifice to the gods; but Alban, undaunted by his menaces, refused to do so, and scourges being found of no more avail than threats to induce him to recant, the governor in a rage ordered him to be immediately beheaded. For this purpose he was taken to a neighbouring hill,* and there the first English martyr sacrificed his life in defence of the Christian faith. The hill that was consecrated by his blood is the very hill where the venerable Abbey, in all its massive grandeur, towers above the town which by its name and traditions perpetuates the memory of the martyr.

* Called Holmhurst by the Saxons.

The account of the martyrdom of St. Alban is thus much easy of belief; but other events related in connection with it, though in olden times readily believed, are looked upon with a smile of incredulity in this sceptical age. It is said that the bridge over the river he had to cross was so narrow that the throng of spectators who crowded to see the execution could not get over it. The saint lifted up his eyes to heaven in prayer, the stream was miraculously divided, and the multitude crossed on dry ground. This wonderful miracle (so runs the legend) awed the mind of the executioner to such a degree that he refused to perform the horrid office, and himself suffered death as the penalty of his disobedience. The venerable Bede graphically tells the story of the martyrdom of St. Alban, and describes the scene of his death :—" The most reverend confessor of God ascended the hill with the throng, the which decently pleasant agreeable place is almost five hundred paces from the river, embellished with several sorts of flowers, or rather quite covered with them, wherein there is no part upright or steep, nor anything craggy, but the sides stretching out far about are levelled by nature like the sea, which of old it had rendered worthy to be enriched with the martyr's blood for its beautiful appearance." On arriving at the top of the hill St. Alban prayed for water to quench his thirst, and immediately a fountain sprang up under his feet. One would have thought that this second miracle would awe the Pagans from their sacrilegious design, but it seemed to have no effect on them, and another executioner having been procured, he at one blow severed the head of the martyr from his body. But the final miracle has yet to be related. The executioner became the victim of Divine vengeance, for as soon as he gave the fatal stroke his eyes dropped out of his head!

Such are the monkish legends to which the death of the proto-martyr of Britain gave rise. But apart from these, very touching and beautiful is the story of the death of St. Alban :—

> " England's first martyr, whom no threats could shake,
> Self-offered victim for his friend he died,
> And for the faith—nor shall his name forsake
> That hill, whose flowery platform seems to rise
> By nature decked for holiest sacrifice."

In an ancient history of St. Albans, quoted by Camden, it is recorded that the citizens of Verulam, as a "disgrace to St. Alban's memory, and as a terror to other Christians, had the story of his murder inscribed upon marble, and inserted in the city walls." But the Christian faith survived the flames of Pagan persecution, and in these early days of Christianity, as in later times, it was true that "the blood of the martyrs is the seed of the Church." Both Bede and Gildas state that a few years after the persecution had subsided a church was founded in honour of St. Alban on the spot on which he suffered martyrdom, where the present Abbey of St. Albans now stands—a grand old memorial of the triumph of Christianity over its foes. The Romano-British Church, which was erected in the time of Constantine, was standing in Bede's time and in that of Offa, the founder of the Abbey.

Tradition records that soon after the martyrdom of St. Alban a large number of the citizens of Verulam went into Wales, in search of Amphibalus, in order to be instructed in Christianity. An army was sent after them, which slew them all, and brought back Amphibalus, whom they put to death at the village of Redbourn, within sight of the city of Verulam.

At the time of the Pelagian heresy, which prevailed A.D 401, Germanus, Bishop of Auxerre, and Lupus, Bishop of Troyes, came into Britain for the purpose of suppressing that heresy, and are said to have assisted at a synod held at Verulam. Germanus, according to tradition, caused the grave of St. Alban to be opened, and deposited therein the relics of other saints which he had brought over with him. A chapel was erected in honour of Germanus on "the spot on which, as from a pulpit, he spoke the Divine word." The ruins of this chapel were in existence at the beginning of the last century, and gave its name to St. German's farm, which includes a great part of the site of Verulam.

For two centuries we have no record in history of the city of Verulam. Some time after the visit of Germanus the city was taken by the Saxons. They were afterwards driven out by the Britons, under Uther Pendragon, but they recovered possession of the city, and are supposed to have murdered the inhabitants, and to have reduced the city to a heap of ruins. It is probable, however, that it was not altogether uninhabited until after the rise of modern St. Albans.

The martyrdom of St. Alban took place, according to Bede, in 286; but according to Usher, in 303. It was not, however, till the eighth century that a religious house was founded in honour of the saint.

CHAPTER II.

King Offa—His resolve to found a Monastery—His search for the relics of the martyr—The miraculous light—The finding of the body of St. Alban—Its removal to a shrine—Offa's journey to Rome—The foundation of the Monastery—The death of Offa and of Willegod, the first abbot—The growth of the Monastery—Vulsig and Vulnoth—The Shrine of St. Alban despoiled—Ulsinus, the founder of the town of St. Albans—Aelfric purchases the King's Fishpool—Ealdred and Eadmer—Excavations at Verulam—Discovery of a History of St. Alban—Leofric and Aelfric the Second—Destruction of the Royal Palace—Leofstan—Watling Street protected from thieves and wild beasts—Abbot Frederick and his opposition to William the Conqueror—Paul, the first Norman Abbot—Rebuilds the Abbey Church—His austerity—D'Albini, fifteenth abbot—Consecration of the Abbey Church—Geoffrey de Gorham—His love of splendour—Founds the Nunnery of Sopwell—Origin of the Liberty of St. Alban.

WE have now to tell of the gradual rise of the town of St. Albans after the final fall of Verulam, and to lay before our readers as concisely as possible an account of the founding of the great monastery, which was reared on the soil that had been hallowed by the blood of the first British martyr. Towards the end of the eighth century, Offa, King of the Mercians, aspiring to obtain possession of East Anglia, invited Ethelbert, the king of that province, to marry his daughter. The unfortunate prince accepted the offer, and visited King Offa's court in order to seek the hand of the princess, but he was there treacherously murdered at the instigation, it was said, of Offa's queen, and East Anglia was annexed by Offa to his own kingdom of Mercia. The foul deed, however, considerably troubled the king's conscience—as well it might—and he was continually haunted by the ghost of the murdered Ethelbert. Offa resolved to set himself right again, in the usual way of crowned heads in those days, by founding a monastery. It is recorded by William of Malmesbury that the king was encouraged in this task by Charlemagne, with whom he held a friendly correspondence. Tradition asserts that in this pious purpose he was assisted by a divine revelation ;—" In the rest and silence of the night he seemed to be accosted by an angel, who admonished him to raise out of the earth the body of the first British martyr, Alban, and place his remains in a shrine with more suitable ornaments." * We are also told that five centuries after the martyrdom "As Offa was searching for the remains of the martyr at Verulam a supernatural light guided him to the spot where they had been deposited, and the body cf the saint was found just as Germanus had placed it 344 years before." The relics were carried in solemn procession, in which were prelates with banners and croziers, and " long files of priests and monks chanting their litanies," and were placed in the little church which had been erected on the spot where Alban suffered. The king placed a circlet of gold round the skull of Alban with the saint's name and title inscribed upon it, and the relics were deposited in a reliquary or shrine, which was inlaid with gold and silver, and richly adorned with precious stones. The building of the monastery was afterwards begun, and so great was the importance attached to the design that, by the advice of his counsellors, Offa set out on a pilgrimage to Rome in order to secure the blessing and assistance of the Pope (Adrian the First) in carrying it into execution. This he succeeded in obtaining. The proto-martyr was canonised by the Pope, and special privileges were granted by the Holy Father to the new abbey. The monastery was to be exempt from episcopal jurisdiction, from the payment of Peter-pence (an annual payment originally granted by Ina, King of the West Saxons, for the maintenance of a Saxon college at Rome), and was allowed to collect and retain for its own use the Peter-pence levied in Hertfordshire. In return, Offa engaged to make perpetual the payment of this tax (which consisted of a penny from every family possessing land of the value of thirty pence), and it con-

* From Matthew Paris, as quoted by Newcome in his "History of St. Albans Abbey."

tinued to be exacted for several centuries. Offa also undertook to maintain a college for English youths at his own expense. On the King's return from Rome, a great council of nobles and prelates was held at Verulam, and the Abbey was erected and munificently endowed. Special revenues were devoted to the exercise of hospitality, and to its gates flocked the poor, the sick, and the wayfarer; nor were any turned empty away. The first stone of the building was laid by Offa, and he appointed a relative of his, named Willegod, to be the first abbot of the new monastery. It was opened for the reception of a hundred monks of the Benedictine order, who were carefully selected from houses of the most regular discipline; and, gradually extending its size and increasing its wealth, it flourished for more than seven centuries, and was governed successively by forty abbots—

"Till Henry's mandate struck the fated shrine,
And sadly closed St. Alban's mitred line."

The royal founder of the Abbey is recorded to have remained at St. Albans till just before his death, busily engaged in the continuation of his pious work, which, though first undertaken as a penance, became to him a labour of love. He died in the year 794, at his palace at Offley, in this county, and was buried at a chapel at Bedford, on the banks of the river Ouse, by which river his sepulchre was afterwards said to have been washed away. Willegod, the first abbot, did not long survive the decease of his royal relative, and his death, two months after, was said to have been partly caused by the grief and mortification he felt at the refusal of Offa's successor to allow the interment of his father's body in the monastery he had founded. *

Of such magnitude did the conventual buildings be-

* Modern research has rendered it extremely doubtful whether Offa carried out his intention of building an entirely new church on the site of the Romano-British Church, described by Bede, which was erected in the days of Constantine by the early converts to Christianity "out of the ancient edifices of the heathen." Sir Gilbert Scott conjectures that it may have "remained incorporated with the Anglo-Saxon Church," round which the monastic buildings were raised, "till the period when the present gigantic structure was erected; and its fragments, indistinguishable from the mass of Roman material of which the church is so largely constructed, may yet form part of its venerable walls."

come "that they more resembled a town than a religious establishment," and "the extent of the monastery was in proportion to its immense estates." "Although," says Newçome, "originally subject to the diocesan, the Lord Abbot gradually advanced in external splendour till the Abbey Church became a rival to the Cathedral," and this "went on until, at the dissolution, the mitred abbots, who had laboured for pre-eminence, outnumbered the bishops in the House of Lords."

The lives of the abbots of St. Albans, as they are chronicled by Matthew Paris (who himself joined the monastery), Walsingham, Amundesham, and others, are full of interest, and they undoubtedly prove that many blessings as well as many evils flowed from the monastic institutions of olden time. "The monastery" (of St. Albans), says Newcombe, "was the house of reception for all the sick, who were here nursed, spiritually consoled, and cured. The monastery generally employed masters to teach the poor children of the neighbourhood; entertained all persons who were ingenious in any art or science; and translated books when few understood the art or could undertake it. There is now extant a chronicle composed and printed at St. Albans in 1484, under the countenance then given to this particular abbey by Richard III." The hospitality of the monks found ample materials for its exercise in the relief of the wants of the many travellers whom its nearness to Watling Street, the great thoroughfare to the north, brought to its gates.

In the interval between its foundation by King Offa and the accession of the first Norman abbot, the monastery was ruled over by thirteen Saxon abbots in succession. The limits of our space will not allow us to do more than make a brief reference to some of them. Vulsig, the third abbot, was no ascetic. He was proud, extravagant, intemperate, fond of hunting, and he practised the "great enormity of inviting crowds of noble ladies to his table." His successor, Vulnoth, though he followed his example to some extent, reformed some of the abuses which had already crept into the monastery, and recovered most of the Abbey land which Vulsig had bestowed upon his own relatives. The reliquary of St. Alban was said to have been broken open by the Danes in the time of Abbot Vulnoth, and some of the bones taken away and conveyed to Denmark, where they were deposited under a costly shrine.

To Ulsinus, the sixth abbot, must be attributed the honour of having been the chief founder and benefactor of the town of St. Albans. Newcome says that " by this time (about the year 950) something of a village was gathered about the new church and abbey." Ulsinus founded the three churches of St. Albans, dedicated to St. Peter, St. Michael, and St. Stephen, at the different entrances to the town. Acting conversely to the modern mode of church extension, he built the churches in order to induce people to live there, and not as the consequence of an increase of population. He " encouraged and invited the inhabitants of the adjacent parts to build and settle in St. Albans, and for that purpose gave them materials and money; and, moreover, laid out and embellished a place for a market." Aelfric, the seventh abbot, won great reputation for his learning and piety. His most memorable act was to exchange a cup of excellent workmanship which Eadfrith had given to the monastery, together with other things of value, for the fishpool situate near St. Michael's bridge, belonging to the Royal manor of Kingsbury, which occasioned great annoyance to the monks, and which he drained of its waters.

Ealdred, the eighth abbot of St. Albans, is represented by Matthew Paris as searching into the ruins of Verulam, carefully and laboriously, and saving all the building materials he could find, in order to use them in the rebuilding of the Abbey Church, but death prevented the accomplishment of his design. His successor, Eadmer, continued the search, and increased the store of materials which had been collected by Ealdred, for the " Church which he proposed to fabricate to the holy martyr Alban." It was not, however, till the Conquest that the materials were employed in the reconstruction of the Abbey Church, and these Roman remains, the *debris* of ancient Verulam, may be seen to have been largely used for that purpose. Eadmer disinterred a number of ruined temples, altars, vases, statues of heathen gods, and urns and ashes, which, as heathen remains, he carefully destroyed in his religious zeal. But in a hollow place in a wall of the buried city an "unknown volume" was found, richly illuminated in gold, and in excellent preservation. On its being examined by a very aged and learned priest, it was found to be no other than a "History of St. Alban," written in ancient British. Having been translated into Latin, in order to be used by the brethren of the convent in their public preachings, we are told that it immediately crumbled into dust.

Leofric and Aelfric, the tenth and eleventh abbots, were two brothers of noble birth, and were men of great piety and benevolence. During the time of Leofric a famine raged in England, and to relieve the general distress the abbot sold many of the treasures belonging to the Abbey. He was afterwards raised to the see of Canterbury, and died in 1006. Aelfric (second of that name) had been chancellor to king Ethelred, and in his own right became possessed of the royal palace of Kingsbury, which he caused to be razed to the ground, leaving only a small tower as a memorial of the regal residence. Leofstan, the twelfth abbot, succeeded Aelfric. He had been the confessor, as well as the familiar friend, of King Edward and his queen, and through his interest with the great he procured various rich grants for the monastery. The most memorable act of this abbot was his endeavour to protect the travellers on the great highway of Watling Street from the attacks of robbers and wild beasts, by cutting down the woods and groves which were their haunts and hiding places, and by granting the manor of Flamstead to a brave knight named Thurnoth, and his two followers, on condition that they should defend travellers from their depredations, and should protect the Church of St. Albans from injury. In this incident we have a picture of the rude and unsettled state of the times.

We now come to the last of the line of Saxon abbots, which ended with the Norman Conquest. In 1066 Frederick (in whose veins ran royal Saxon blood) was installed Abbot of St. Albans. After the Battle of Hastings William the Conqueror marched to Berkhamstead, there to receive the submission of the Saxon nobles. The king afterwards proceeded to Westminster, where he was crowned, and then started on a journey to St. Albans. The Abbot Frederick, who refused to acknowledge William, prevented his visit to St. Albans by causing great trees to be felled and laid across the road to impede his march, and having placed himself at the head of the discontented nobles, with the object of raising *Engelondes Dereling*, the exiled Edgar Atheling, to the throne, became especially the object of the king's anger; and he was obliged to leave St. Albans, and take refuge in the monastery of Ely, where he died, it is said, of grief and mortification. As might be expected, St. Albans suffered for the brave conduct of its abbot. William seized a great part of the Abbey lands, and but for the entreaties of Lanfranc he would have destroyed the monastery. Lanfranc obtained the appointment of Paul, a relation of his, who had come over with him from Normandy, and who thus became the fourteenth abbot.

Paul, the first Norman abbot, was appointed in 1077, eleven years after the Conquest. With the aid of Lanfranc, who contributed a thousand marks towards the undertaking, he rebuilt the Abbey Church, which had been allowed to fall into ruin, and all the monastic buildings, except the bakehouse and the mill-house. His materials were the tiles and stones of ancient Verulam, and the timber collected by his predecessors. Abbot Paul introduced a severer system of discipline than had previously existed in the monastery, so that " under him," says Walsingham, " St. Albans Abbey became a school of religious observance for all England." The Abbey rapidly rose in repute for sanctity, and Abbot Paul obtained many new benefactions to it, as well as the restitution of the manors of Redbourn and Childwick, which had been alienated from it.

Paul died in 1093, and for four years after the king (William Rufus) held the Abbey in his own hands, and appropriated the revenue. He then appointed Richard de Aubeney, or de Albini. The new church was consecrated with great pomp and ceremony at Christmas time, 1115, during his abbacy. The king and queen (Henry the First and Matilda), with many nobles, abbots, and prelates, were present, and during eleven days were entertained at the cost of the Abbey.

On the death of Richard de Albini, in 1119, he was succeeded by Geoffrey de Gorham, the sixteenth abbot, who greatly improved the internal regulations of the monastery, increased the size of the Abbey buildings, and multiplied its revenues. He seems to have been possessed in a large degree of that passion for pomp and outward splendour which was so prominent a characteristic of mediæval times. It is recorded that he provided rich vessels and splendid garments for the various services of the church, and, more than that, he prepared a very magnificent shrine for the relics of St. Alban.* The remains of the martyr were removed with great solemnity from the ancient tomb, and were exhibited for the inspection of all present. Abbot Geoffrey also founded the Nunnery of Sopwell, and to the rule of this abbot may be traced the origin of the Liberty of St. Alban, which ancient jurisdiction was, in 1875, fused with that of the county of Hertford. Henry the First conferred on the abbot the power of holding pleas and of taking cognisance of all lesser crimes and offences which had been punishable in the leets, the hundreds, and the county courts.†

* This shrine, in which the remains of St. Alban were placed in 1129, was said to have been made of the most costly materials (gold, silver, and precious stones), and Matthew Paris, who gave an elaborate description of it, declared it to be more splendid than any other he ever beheld.
† Newcome's "History."

CHAPTER III.

Robert de Gorham, eighteenth abbot—Obtains privileges and immunities for the Monastery from Pope Adrian—Gorhambury—Abbot Symon—Warren de Cambridge, twentieth abbot—Abbot John de Cella—Rebuilds the west end of the Church—William de Trumpington, twenty-second abbot—Finishes the west end of the Church—King John and the Barons—Abbot John, of Hertford—Royal visits—Matthew Paris—Roger de Norton, twenty-fourth abbot—Dispute between the abbot and the townspeople—The Constable of Hertford is beheaded—Queen Eleanor's Cross—Hugh de Eversden, twenty-seventh abbot—His contentions with the townspeople—Erects the Lady Chapel—Abbot Wallingford—His successful defence of ecclesiastical domination—Michael de Mentmore, twenty-ninth abbot—A Royal Baptism—The King of France brought to St. Albans—Wat Tyler's Insurrection—The abbot beautifies the Church and rebuilds the great gate—John of Wheathamstead, thirty-third abbot—Repairs the Abbey fabric—Humphrey, Duke of Gloucester—The abbot evades the Mortmain Act—Abbot Stoke—Burial of Duke Humphrey—Re-election of Abbot Wheathamstead.

THE accession of the eighteenth abbot, Robert de Gorham (1151) marks an important period in the history of the monastery. He was the first abbot on whom the mitre was conferred, and the abbots of St. Albans were authorised by Pope Adrian IV. (Nicholas Brekespeare) to take precedence of all others in England. This Pope, who was the only Englishman that ever sat in the chair of St. Peter, was born at Abbot's Langley, in Hertfordshire. It is recorded that in his youth he was refused admission to the monastery of St. Albans on the ground of insufficiency of learning; but the recollection of this rebuff did not deter him from restoring to the Abbey its ancient privilege of exemption from all eclesiastical jurisdiction except that of the Pope himself. King Stephen was royally entertained by Robert de Gorham, and this abbot renewed and re-adorned the Feretory of St. Albans, which had been despoiled in the time of his predecessor to supply the wants of the poor during a famine. He conferred many gifts on his relatives, the chief of which were some lands in the neighbourhood that were left to one of his family, and were called after his name—"the lands of Gorham," or "Gorhambury," the name which the estate in the possession of the Earl of Verulam still bears.

After the death of Robert de Gorham, the king for some time refused to allow a successsor to be appointed. The arrogance of Thomas à Becket having reached an intolerable point, Henry was resolved to appoint high dignitaries in the Church without the interference of the haughty prelate, or even of the Pope himself; and he appointed Symon, the prior of the monastery, to the dignity of abbot. Symon, who was nineteenth abbot, had a comparatively mild and peaceful rule. He enriched and completed the shrine of St. Alban, which Abbot Geoffrey had reared. This abbot was distinguished by his learning and love of literature, and he procured copies of the best books for the use of his monastery. Amongst these were the Old and New Testaments. The supposed relics of St. Amphibalus, the "instructor and pastor of St. Alban," were found at Redbourn during the rule of this abbot. The Abbot Symon died in 1183, and was succeeded by Warren de Cambridge, the twentieth abbot. In the time of this abbot the Bishop of Lincoln made an abortive attempt to recover episcopal jurisdiction over the monastery, which his predecessor had consented to relinquish. The abbot appealed to the king, but the king with much anger refused the request, which the bishop never afterwards dared to renew.

John de Cella, the twenty-first abbot, was born at Markyate Cell, in the parish of Caddington. This abbot, soon after his accession, began to enlarge and reconstruct the west end of the church, in accordance with the will of Abbot Warren, who bequeathed a hundred marks for that purpose. These were expended, however, long before the new foundations had been raised to the level of the ground; the work was carried on very slowly, and in spite of many obstacles; and John de Cella found himself unable to finish what he had begun. It was at this period that the western part of the church, which was of Norman, began to be changed to its present more rich and beautiful style. The abbot imposed a tax of one sheaf of corn to be given annually for every acre sown on the Abbey estates. This tax was levied for twenty-four years. During the rule of this abbot the Pope placed the kingdom under an interdict. King John required the abbot to disobey the interdict by continuing the ordinary religious services. The abbot refused to comply with the king's command, and thereupon his majesty took possession of the monastery, and turned out the monks. The abbot only recovered possession by payment of one hundred marks, and five hundred more were afterwards exacted from him. One of the expedients resorted to for obtaining money to complete the Abbey would scarcely be approved in these days. The abbot sent a man to go about the country pretending he had been raised from the dead by St. Alban and St. Amphibalus, and that he was able to give proof of their miracles. By this pious fraud large sums of money were collected from the simple-minded and credulous people of that age. Abbot John, however, died in the odour of sanctity, and it was even recorded of him that when he sang alone the responses were made by angels!

William de Trumpington, the twenty-second abbot (1214-1235) completed the west front of the Abbey Church with its roofs and arches, decorated the windows in the aisles, heightened the towers, and restored and enlarged St. Cuthbert's Chapel, which had been built by Richard de Albini, whose withered arm was said to have been miraculously restored by touching the saint's remains. Abbot Trumpington modified, however, the details of his predecessor's work in a very reckless manner, and impoverished his design in order to lessen the cost. During his great contest with the barons, King John retired to the monastery, where he convened a council of his followers, in the hope of regaining the power he had lost by signing Magna Charta. William appears to have been a man of great discretion and worldly wisdom, and notwithstanding the stormy times in which he lived, he preserved the peace of the monastery, increased its revenues, was lamented at his death, and was buried with much pomp and ceremony.

During the rule of the twenty-third abbot, John of

Hertford, who was appointed in 1235, Henry III. repeatedly visited the monastery, and made several costly presents in return for the hospitality he received. The east end of the church was rebuilt during the rule of this abbot. In the year 1259, the Abbey lost its illustrious member, Matthew Paris, the historian, who was called "the pride and glory of the monastery." Matthew Paris entered the monastery during the rule of Abbot William, and his Lives of the Abbots of St. Albans conclude with that of John of Hertford, who died in 1260.

The twenty-fourth abbot was Roger de Norton, in whose time the church and monastery were beautified and enlarged at a considerable cost. In 1264 a tumult arose between the townspeople and the abbot concerning the Abbey mills. The former denied the abbot's right to force them to full their cloth and grind their corn at his mills, on his own terms. During the commotion Gregory de Stokes, the Constable of Hertford, ventured into the town, with three attendants, and in consequence of their insolent behaviour, they were seized and beheaded by the exasperated townspeople, for which outrage the king compelled them to pay a penalty of one hundred marks. The dispute was decided in favour of the abbot, who, however, promised to be in future more moderate in his charges for the use of his mills.

St. Albans was one of the places in which the body of Queen Eleanor rested on its way to London from Herdeby, a town near Lincoln; and here, therefore, a stately cross was erected by Edward the First. In the Corporation records is the following entry:—" Ordered that a market-house be built and set up where the cross lately stood "

Hugh de Eversden, the twenty-seventh abbot, had to contend with the people for his privileges, who were beginning to know their strength and to struggle successfully for their liberties against sacerdotal oppression, as well as against the despotism of the civil power. The inhabitants of St. Albans rebelled against the heavy yoke of the abbot, and obtained from the king a writ, commanding the abbot "to place all the liberties, privileges, and franchises of the town on the same establishment as was recorded in Domesday Book." The abbot ultimately signed a deed, restoring to the burgesses of the borough the power of returning two representatives to Parliament, and other rights of which they had been deprived. The abbot died in 1326, unregretted by the monks, who never forgave him for his concessions to the townsmen, and he left the monastery heavily burdened with the debt which he had contracted in the erection of the beautiful Lady Chapel, and by his profuse expenditure.

Richard de Wallingford, twenty-eighth abbot (a blacksmith's son), was a bold defender of ecclesiastical assumption, and he succeeded in obtaining a formal surrender of all the privileges the townspeople had wrested from Hugh de Eversden, with all their charters and records.* Abbot Wallingford was well versed in the sciences of mathematics and astronomy, and he constructed an astronomical clock called Albion, which was said to be the wonder of the age.

The fifth son of Edward the Third was born at King's Langley, in 1341, and was baptised by Abbot de Mentmore (twenty-ninth abbot) in the royal palace there. The child was named Edward de Langley. The queen in due time came to the Abbey, and made an offering of a cloth of gold of great value. This abbot made many new regulations for the better government of the monastery. At the middle of the fourteenth century the religious orders throughout England had grown extremely dissolute and corrupt, and the Abbey of St. Albans was no exception to the rule. Abbot de Mentmore renewed the attempts at reform which were begun by his predecessor, and were continued by his successor, Thomas de la Mare, the thirtieth abbot. This abbot was in high favour with the king (Edward the Third), who made him president of the general chapter of Benedictines throughout England. After the battle of Poictiers (in 1356), John, King of France, who was made captive in the battle by Edward the Black Prince, was taken to St. Albans and placed in the monastery, in the custody of the abbot, who treated him with great dignity and humanity.

The formidable insurrection (headed by Wat Tyler and Jack Straw) which took place in the fourth year of the reign of Richard the Second (1381), placed in peril the rights

* Walsingham MSS.

and privileges of the Abbey, and even threatened the entire destruction of the monastery. A number of rebels, under the command of Jack Straw, came to St. Albans, and were reinforced by some of the disaffected townspeople; amongst the latter was one Grindcoble, who had been in the service of the abbot. Under threats of violence they extorted a number of concessions from de la Mare. Their success emboldened the inhabitants of most of the manors belonging to the Abbey to put in various claims to privileges and exemptions, which the abbot prudently granted, knowing full well that when the royal authority was completely re-established, these concessions could be easily retracted. After the insurrection had been quelled, the king himself came down to St. Albans, with the Chief Justice, to try the ringleaders, and eighteen of them were executed and hung in chains. The king stayed at the Abbey eight days, and caused "all the commons of the county," between the ages of fifteen and sixty, to take the oath of fidelity to him in the great court of the Abbey.

Peace having been restored, Abbot de la Mare set about adorning the church " much more richly than any of his predecessors had ever done." He rebuilt the great gate of the Abbey (which had been blown down by a high wind), " with its chambers, its prisons, and its vaults, and the roof covered with lead."* Abbot de la Mare died in 1396, at the ripe age of eighty-eight.

John of Wheathamstead, the thirty-third abbot, was the most illustrious in this long line of mitred priests. He was intimately connected in friendship with many high and noble persons in the land, and he used his influence with them to obtain large sums of money for the repair of the Abbey fabric, which had fallen into decay through the neglect of his predecessors. To this end he revived an ancient practice of admitting distinguished persons as lay and honorary members of the monastery. In 1423 the great Humphrey, Duke of Gloucester, was so admitted, with Jaquelini his wife. It appears that John, in common with many other ecclesiastics, had recourse to various subter-

* This refers to the building which was for many years used as the Liberty Gaol and House of Correction. It was a prison in the time of de la Mare. The abbots had a civil as well as an ecclesiastical jurisdiction, and could, therefore, try and punish ordinary offences against the law.

fuges for the purpose of evading the provisions of the Mortmain Act which forbad the extortion of death-bed legacies to the enormous revenues of the Church or of the various monastic bodies. To render himself quite secure, he obtained the royal pardon for his disobedience of this law of Mortmain, and this was confirmed by Parliament. In 1440, in view of the distractions which threatened the country, and of the decay of the influence and fortunes of his best friend, Humphrey, Duke of Gloucester, he resigned his office, after a rule of twenty years.

John Stoke, the thirty-fourth abbot, was chosen in the room of Wheathamstead. The principal event in his time was the death (in 1447) of Duke Humphrey, who was found dead in his bed the night after he had been consigned to prison. "His body was," says an ancient chronicle, " showed by the Lords and Commons as though he had died of a palsey. But all indifferent persons well knew that he died of no natural death, but of some violent force." The body of this illustrious man was interred in the Abbey Church, where a beautiful monument was erected to his memory by Abbot Stoke. John Stoke died in 1451. Wheathamstead was again elected abbot, and continued to govern the monastery till 1462. Had he foreseen that the fierce struggle between the Houses of York and Lancaster would reach its bloody height in two battles fought in the immediate vicinity of St. Albans, he would probably have refused to assume again the high ecclesiastical dignity he had voluntarily resigned.

CHAPTER IV.

The Wars of the Roses—The first battle of St. Albans—Defeat of the King's army—The abbot counsels moderation—The second battle of St. Albans—Defeat of the Yorkists—Re-union of the king and queen—Plunder of the town—The Earl of March proclaimed king—A royal charter—William Wallingford, thirty-sixth abbot—Erects the altar screen—Introduction of the Art of Printing—Abbot Ramryge—Cardinal Wolsey—The beginning of the end—A commission appointed by the King—Richard Boreman, fortieth and last abbot—His surrender of the Abbey—Dissolution of the Monastery.

THE battles fought at St. Albans during the Wars of the Roses, the incidents of which must have presented so terrible a contrast to the even tenour of monastic life, are, of course, familiar to the student of history. The first battle of St. Albans was fought on the 23rd of May, 1455, between King Henry the Sixth and Richard, Duke of York. The meek and irresolute king, who pathetically exclaimed that "he had fallen upon evil days," set forth from Westminster with an army of two thousand men on the 21st of May, and quartered that night at Watford. His object was to stop the progress of the Duke of York, who was marching from the north with a body of three thousand men. Early the next morning the king came to St Albans and fixed his standard in St. Peter's Street. The Duke of York encamped at a place called Key Field, on the east side of the town. The cry amongst the Yorkists was "Give up the Duke of Somerset." This nobleman had been impeached of treason in the House of Commons, and committed to the Tower, from which he was released by the influence of the queen. The king's force had barricaded the town on the side next the Yorkists, and the Royalists held their position so bravely that a vigorous assault, made by the Duke of York, on the town at St. Peter's Street was successfully repulsed. A strong party, however, headed by the Earl of Warwick, broke into the town by the garden side, between the sign of the Key and the Exchequer, in Holywell Street,* and shouting "A Warwick! a Warwick!" they fiercely attacked the Royalists. The impetuosity of the onslaught, and the terror inspired by the name of Warwick, overcame the force opposed to him, and after a dreadful conflict in the streets of the town, the royal army lost heart and fled. The king, finding himself deserted and alone, and wounded in the neck by an arrow, took refuge in a small cottage occupied by a baker. There he was found by the Duke of York, who, with all show of courtesy, conducted the crestfallen and unhappy king to the Abbey, and the next day to London. The sacrifice of life on the king's side amounted to about eight hundred men, among whom were many persons of distinction—the Duke of Somerset, the Earls of Strafford and Northumberland, Lord Clifford, and many others. About six hundred of the Yorkists were slain. After the battle the duke's men began to plunder the town. The abbot, in order to propitiate them, sent them out great quantities of victuals and wine, and by command of the Duke of York, they refrained from plundering or injuring in any way the Abbey and its inmates. After their obsequies had been solemnly performed, the bodies of the principal nobles were interred in the Chapel of the Virgin. The remains of some other persons of distinction, and of the common soldiers, were consigned to St. Peter's.

The rule of Abbot Wheathamstead was rendered still more memorable by the second battle of St. Albans, which was fought on Shrove Tuesday, the 17th of February, 1461, between Margaret of Anjou, queen of Henry the Sixth, and the Yorkists, under the command of the Earl of Warwick. The queen had gained a decisive victory at Wakefield, in Yorkshire, where the Duke of York had been slain; but the Yorkists still continued to contest his claim to the throne, in the person of his son, Edward, Earl of March. The queen, encouraged by her victory, marched towards the metropolis, and the Earl of Warwick, carrying the king

* The spot thus described was, no doubt, that between the Cross Keys Inn and what is now called the Queen's Hotel, in Chequer Street, formerly the Exchequers.

with him, left London with a strong force to meet her. The queen encamped her army on Bernard Heath, on the north-east side of the town of St. Albans. The Yorkists entered the town on the opposite side by the Dunstable Road, and, meeting the queen's troops in the market-place, they attacked them, and "with a storm of arrows which flew as thick as hail," drove them back to the heath, whither they were hotly pursued by the Yorkists. For some time victory inclined to neither side; but at length the Yorkists were compelled to give way—a panic spread through their ranks, and, though they were far superior in numbers, they were utterly routed by the queen's troops. There is a great disparity in the records of the estimated loss of life in this battle. According to Stow, 1,916 men were slain; but according to Hollinshead, 230. The only person of distinction who was killed in this battle was one Sir John Gray, who had been knighted, with twelve others, by the king on the preceding day, in "the town of Colney," After the battle the king sent a message to the "Northern lords," assuring them of his regard for them, and he was conducted by Sir Thomas Hoo to the tent of Lord Clifford, where he had a joyful meeting with the queen and the Prince of Wales. The royal party afterwards went to the Abbey, and were received "with hymns and songs" by the abbot and monks. They were then led before the high altar to return thanks for the queen's victory, thence to the shrine of St. Alban, and finally to the royal chamber. At the entreaty of the abbot, a proclamation was issued by the king and queen, with a view to restrain the northern men, of whom the queen's army was chiefly composed, from plundering the town. But as the queen had previously promised them the plunder and spoil of their enemies, this proclamation was of no avail; "and," says Chauncey, "they spared not anything they found that was fit for them to carry away." These excesses greatly damaged the queen's cause. The approach of the Earl of March, and the evident disaffection of the inhabitants of London, induced her to leave St. Albans for the north again. Not long after the Earl of March was proclaimed king under the title of Edward IV. Our discreet Abbot Wheathamstead ingratiated himself with the new king, who granted a charter which added very much to the civil power of the abbots, "within their towns of St. Albans, Watford, and Barnet: and also the hundred of Cashio and all their whole Liberty of St. Alban." By this charter the cognisance of the gravest offences and full power of life and death were given to the abbots. Abbot Wheathamstead died in 1464, and was buried in the chapel he himself had erected.

William Wallingford, the thirty-sixth abbot, was elected in 1476. In the rule of this abbot the beautiful altar screen was erected which is called after his name. One of the most important events in the history of the monastery marked the rule of Wallingford, and that was its connection with the introduction into England of an art which heralded a new era in the history of the world. It is a fact of which the townspeople of St. Albans may be proud that St. Albans was one of the first places in which the art of printing was practised in this country. Literature and the fine arts had, ever since the spread of Christianity in Great Britain, been fostered and developed at St. Albans; and it was therefore fitting that the invention of the printing press should early find an asylum in its monastery. Little dreamt the monks, who looked on with wonder as CAXTON plied his art within the walls of Westminster Abbey, what a mighty revolution that rude printing press had ushered into the world. It is a remarkable fact that the Abbeys of Westminster and St. Albans should have been the first homes, and their monks the earliest patrons, of the new art. The first book known to have been printed by Caxton in this country is dated 1474; and in 1480 was published the earliest book printed at St. Albans Abbey. It was entitled *Rhetorica Nova Fratris Laurencii Gulielmi de Saona*. Of this book there are three copies extant. Two other works appeared the same year. In 1481 was published *In Aristotelis Physica, lib* viii,; and in 1483 *The St. Albans Chronicle* was compiled and "also emprynted by one, sometimes scole master of St. Albans." There are two copies of the work extant. But the most remarkable of the works which issued from the printing press here was the celebrated book, since called "The Gentleman's Recreation," printed in 1486, and chiefly compiled by the

Prioress of Sopwell Nunnery, Dame Juliana Berners. The work consists of three treatises—one on hawking, another on hunting and fishing, and the third on coat armour. The printer was a monk of the Abbey.

Wallingford died in 1484. He was succeeded by Thomas Ramryge, the thirty-seventh abbot, who, however, was not appointed till 1492. The only memorial left of him is his magnificent shrine in the choir of the Abbey Church. The records relative to this abbot and his times Newcome supposes were destroyed at the dissolution of the monastery in 1539.

Upon the death of Ramryge, Cardinal Wolsey, then Bishop of Winchester, Archbishop of York, Chancellor of England, and the Pope's Legate, was appointed to take the Abbey *in commendam*. This was the beginning of the end. Wolsey applied the revenues of the monastery to the formation of the colleges at Oxford and Ipswich, which was considered to be a most serious violation of the canon law of the realm. When Wolsey fell, he was convicted under the statute of Præmunire, and all his property was declared to be forfeited to the Crown. On his obtaining a pardon, he was allowed to retain till his death the title of Abbot of St. Albans, the king himself appropriating the revenues. Wolsey died in September, 1530, and Robert Catton became the thirty-ninth abbot, and continued in the abbacy till the year 1538, when two commissioners were appointed to visit the Abbey, and report on its condition. The abbot, however, refused to submit tamely to the wishes of the king, who was eager to seize on the possessions and revenues of the monastery, though his bold opposition was unavailing. It is supposed that Catton died in the year 1538.

Richard Boreman de Stevenache, the fortieth and last abbot, was initiated with the understanding that he should make a peaceable surrender of the monastery and its revenues. On the 5th December, 1539, the king's commissioners came down to the Abbey, when Boreman signed a deed of surrender, and delivered up the seal of the monastery.* As a compensation to the Abbot for this

---

* This seal, which is now in the British Museum, is made of ivory. It represents St. Alban, holding in his hand a branch of the palm tree.

sacrifice, the king granted him by charter a yearly pension of £266 13s. 4d. To the prior he gave a yearly pension of £33 6s. 8d., and the remaining monks, thirty-eight in number, were also pensioned. The revenues of the monastery were estimated at this time, by Stow, at £2,500; and at £2,100 by Dugdale. Most of the possessions of the now dissolved monastery were bestowed on the king's favourite courtiers. The monastic buildings, with all the land adjacent, and the parish church of St. Andrew, which stood on the north side of the Abbey, were granted by the king to Sir Richard Lee, Knight, in February, 1539—40, and the buildings were afterwards ruthlessly demolished with the exception of the Gate House. This grant, however, did not include the conventual church, which was subsequently bestowed by charter of King Edward the Sixth to the inhabitants of St. Albans, for the sum of £400, and was made the parish church instead of the church of St. Andrew, which had been pulled down.

So came to an end the monastery of St. Albans. Through long centuries it had flourished and grown, had passed through viccissitudes and triumphs, had become great in the favour of popes, and kings, and prelates, and nobles, and rich in the magnitude of its endowments. But it "had its day, and ceased to be," leaving behind it in the stately Abbey Church the only remaining monument of its ancient renown.

The evils of the monastic system were many and great; but was it not, in its best days, the fountain-head of religious life in England, the fosterer of the arts and sciences, the home of learning, the source of large-hearted charity, of princely munificence, of noble self-devotion?

CHAPTER V.

The Borough of St. Albans—Domesday Book—Charters of Richard I. and Edward VI.—Successive Charters granted by Mary and Elizabeth—The Grammar School and Wine Licenses—Charters of James I., Charles I., Charles II. and James II.—The latter declared void—The Municipal Reform Act.

THE Borough of St. Albans is spoken of in Domesday Book as belonging to the Abbot and Convent of St. Albans, who held it of the king *in capite*. Richard the First granted a charter by which he confirmed to God and the Church of St. Alban the town of St. Albans, with the market, and all the liberty usually belonging to a borough. We have already spoken of the deprivation by the abbots of St. Albans of the rights of the burgesses; of the grant by Abbot Hugh de Eversden (in the reign of Edward the Second) of a charter, giving them power to return two members to Parliament; and of their subsequent surrender of the charter, with all the privileges it conferred. The constitution of the borough remained the same as before until the dissolution of the monastery, when the town, with the profits of fairs, tolls, and other sources of revenue, came to the crown. Edward the Sixth, by a charter dated the 12th of May, 1553, re-incorporated the town of St. Albans, and vested in the Corporation the privileges and revenues which had reverted to the king. The government was vested in the mayor and ten burgesses; and the mayor and inhabitants of the borough were empowered to choose two burgesses to serve in Parliament, there having been no return since the reign of Edward the Third. The charter instituted a market every Wednesday and Saturday (except the week of Christmas), and three fairs—on the Annunciation of the Blessed Virgin Mary, on St. Alban's Day, and on St. Michael's Day—beginning at noon at the vigils of these days, and ending with the noon of the days following these feasts. Of the markets, the market on Wednesday is discontinued; and of the fairs, the Lady Day and Michaelmas fairs, for cattle only are still annually held. By this charter the Justices of the Peace for the Liberty of St. Alban were allowed to have a gaol within the borough, for the safe custody of felons and malefactors taken within the liberty, but out of the borough. The mayor and burgesses were empowered to erect a grammar school in the Church of St. Alban, * and to make statutes for its government.

In consideration of the sum of £400, which had been paid to the king, it was ordained in this charter that " the late monastery of St. Albans shall be called the parish church of the borough, for all the inhabitants within the late parish or chapelry of St. Andrew," and George Wetherall, clerk, was appointed first rector of the Church of St. Alban, for the term of his natural life. Upon this charter being granted, a coat of arms was given to the borough—*Azure, a saltire Or.*

A new charter, confirming the charter of Edward the Sixth, was granted by Queen Mary, dated the 10th of December, 1553; and Queen Elizabeth, in a charter dated the 7th of February, 1559—60, confirmed both the former charters. On the 24th of March, 1569—70, the queen granted another charter at Gorhambury, upon the petition of Sir Nicholas Bacon, knight, lord keeper, which, for the support of the Grammar School founded by Edward the Sixth, gave power to the mayor and burgessses to grant two wine licenses for the borough, on condition that a

---

* *Infra ecclesiam Sancti Albani.* The Lady Chapel was converted into a school-room in pursuance of this charter, and continued to be put to this use until the year 1871, when the grammar school was removed to the building (the gatehouse of the ancient monastery) which was formerly the Liberty Gaol.

salary of twenty pounds a year should be paid by them to
the master of the school ; and that no one should be allowed
to sell wine within the borough but the holders of such
licenses. James the First, by a charter dated the 10th
of May, 1610, granted another wine license, on condition
that four marks should be paid yearly to the mayor and
burgesses, as an augmentation of the salary of the master
of the grammar school. The mayor and burgesses were
authorised to seize any wine sold in the borough, or within
two miles of it, contrary to the tenour of this grant, and to
imprison the offender. *

Another charter was granted by Charles the First, the
17th of December, 1632. This charter determined the
limits of the borough, appointed twenty-five assistants to
the mayor and burgesses, and created the offices of high
steward and recorder, coroner, and town clerk, with other
provisions. In the following year a body of laws,
ordinances, and constitutions (founded upon this charter)
were drawn up for the internal government of the borough.

In the reign of Charles the Second yet another charter
was granted (the 29th of July, 1664), by which the corporation was made to consist of "the mayor, aldermen, and
burgesses of the Borough of St. Albans," and a Common
Council was appointed, consisting of the mayor and twelve
aldermen. In the last year of the same reign, the mayor
and aldermen voluntarily surrendered all their charters and
possessions into the hands of the king ; but the surrender
was invalid because it was never enrolled. The last charter
to the borough was granted by James the Second, the 16th
of March, 1685, but was afterwards declared void, and the
previous charter continued in force. † In common with
other municipal bodies, the corporation was reconstituted
by the Municipal Reform Act of 1835. It now consists of
four aldermen and twelve councillors.

* For a long time this chartered monopoly of wine licenses (without the
consent of Parliament) was disputed. In 1804 a suit was begun in the
Exchequer Court by the Attorney-General against Ann Marks, for
penalties incurred under the charters, and the court decided in confirmation
of the privileges given to the corporate body by these charters. The
wine licenses are still let by contract for a term of three years by the
corporation.

† Some of the original charters are still in possession of the corporation.

CHAPTER VI.

St. Albans in Olden Time—the Martyrdom of Tankerfield—the High Sheriff of Herts, with his retinue, taken prisoners by Oliver Cromwell —Town improvements—Disfranchisement of St. Albans.

ON the history of St. Albans after the dissolution of the monastery, we must not dwell with much minuteness. There is ample proof that by this time the town had acquired considerable size and importance. Its situation on the great highway between London and the North became the source of its prosperity. In the good old coaching days it was a first-rate postal town—famous for its hostelries, and familiar enough to travellers. These were its palmy days, when the perpetual rumble of the stage coaches, the smart crack of the coachman's whip, and the cheerful sound of the bugle horn fell on the ear from morn till night. An idea may be formed of the extent of the traffic on this highway in olden times, from a proverbial expression which Shakespeare uses in the second part of *King Henry IV*, (act i., scene 2), where Poins, in answer to the Prince's remark about Doll Tearsheet, says, " I warrant you, as common as the way between St. Albans and London."

In the reign of Queen Mary, St. Albans was again the scene of a martyrdom, Its first martyr fell a victim to the blind fury of Pagan superstition; its second to the no less cruel rage of Popish intolerance. In the year 1555, George Tankerfield, having become a Protestant, was tried by Bishop Bonner, and after every effort had been made without success to induce him to renounce his heretical opinions, he was condemned to be burned alive. He was brought to St. Albans by the High Sheriff of Hertfordshire, Edward Broket, Esq., and Mr. Puller, of Hitchin, who was under-sheriff.

"They put up at the Cross Keys Inn, where there was a great concourse of people to see and hear the prisoner; some were sorry to find so pious a man brought to be burned; others praised God for his constancy and perseverance in the truth. . . And all this time," continues the Chronicle, "the sheriffs were at a gentleman's house at dinner, not far from the town, whither also resorted many knights and gentlemen out of the country, because his son was married that day, and until they returned from dinner the prisoner was left to the care of his host, by whom he was kindly treated; and considering that his time was short, his saying was—

'Although the day be ever so long,
Yet at last it ringeth to even song.'

"About two o'clock, when the sheriffs returned from dinner, they brought Mr. Tankerfield out of the inn to the place where he should suffer, which was called Rome-land, being a green place near the west end of the Abbey Church, into which when he was come he kneeled down by the stake that was set up for him, and after he had ended his prayers he arose, and, with a joyful faith, said that, although he had a sharp dinner, yet he hoped to have a joyful supper in heaven. While the faggots were set about him, there came a priest and persuaded him to believe in the sacrament of the altar and he would be saved. But Tankerfield cried vehemently, 'I defy the whore of Babylon! fie on the abominable idol; good people, do not believe him.' Then the mayor of the town recommended fire to be set to the heretic, and said if he had but one load of faggots in the world he would give them to burn him. Amidst this confusion, there was a certain knight, who went unto Tankerfield, and, taking him by the hand, said, 'Good brother, be strong in Christ,' This he spoke softly, and Tankerfield said, 'O sir, I am so, thank God.' Then fire was set unto him, and he desired the sheriff and all the people to pray for him. Most of them did so, and so, embracing the fire, he called on the name of the Lord Jesus, and was quickly out of pain." *

An historical incident in the great "Rebellion" must have a notice here. In March, 1643, Charles the First issued a proclamation in which the Earl of Essex, the Parliamentary army, and "all aiders and abettors of the same" were denounced as traitors. The High Sheriff of Hertfordshire being himself an ardent royalist, hastened—with a great deal more zeal than discretion—to the market-place at St. Albans, there to publish the proclamation. Scarcely had the cry of "God save the King" died away, when the ever vigilant Cromwell, with the wonderful celerity and decisiveness which characterised his movements, dashed into the town with a troop of horse, and after a slight resistance on the part of an unarmed and defenceless retinue, took the astonished and baffled sheriff, with his *posse*, into custody, among whom were the Mayor of St. Albans and the

* "Foxe's Book of Martyr's." The spot where Tankerfield suffered is on a plot of ground (lying between the old Abbey gateway and the street) which is now a burial ground for the Abbey parish.

other members of the Corporation. He then sent them all away to London. The House of Commons committed the unfortunate high sheriff to the Tower, and we presume that the Mayor and Corporation were set at liberty.

At the beginning of the present century, the town of St. Albans underwent a number of improvements. One of the chief of these was the formation of a new road through the south-east part of the town, called the New London Road, in place of the old road, which begins in Sopwell Lane, Holywell Hill. By the Reform Act of 1832 the boundaries of the borough were rectified and extended, and by the Municipal Corporations Reform Act the Parliamentary and municipal boundaries were made co-extensive. The trade and importance of St. Albans suffered severely by the revolution in travelling which followed the growth of the railway system. Until the year 1858 St. Albans had no railway communication nearer than Hatfield, on the Great Northern Railway, and Watford and Boxmoor, on the London and North Western Railway. In the year 1858 a branch line of railway from St. Albans to Watford, and in the year 1865 a branch line from St. Albans to Hatfield, were opened. The Midland main line passes through St. Albans, the extension from Bedford to London having been completed in 1868, so that the town now possesses exceptional advantages as a centre of railway communication.

In the year 1852 St. Albans was disfranchised. Flagrant bribery and corruption had for many years prevailed at the borough elections, but not more than in other constituencies which escaped punishment, though perhaps with less prudence and concealment. These corrupt practices had increased to so great an extent that it was felt an example must be made, and so the unfortunate boroughs of Sudbury and St. Albans were fixed upon as scapegoats for the rest of the guilty constituencies. In November, 1850, Mr. Raphael, one of the two members for St. Albans, died, and the candidates for the vacant seat were Mr. Jacob Bell and Mr. Alderman Carden. Mr. Carden contested the borough on "purity principles," which his agents, however, did not carry out in their integrity, and he polled 147 votes, while his opponent, Mr.

Bell, polled 276. Mr. Bell was therefore elected. A petition was presented against his return, which was unsuccessful; but in 1851 an Act of Parliament received the royal assent for appointing royal commissioners to inquire into the existence of bribery in the borough. The commissioners appointed were Sir Frederick William Slade, Q.C., Mr. William Forsyth, and Mr. Thomas Phinn. The commission was opened in the Town Hall, St. Albans, on the 29th October, 1851, and finally closed on the 26th of January 1852. The commissioners reported that in addition to the two recognised parties of Conservatives and Liberals, there was "another of no fixed politics, who called themselves the 'third party,' whose custom it was at all elections where there appeared no probability of a contest, to hang up a key in different parts of the town, as a sign to the electors that a candidate would be brought down to open the borough," The voters belonging to this party were invariably bribed, and were powerful enough to turn the scale on behalf of the candidate who was willing to pay them best. " In truth," says the report, " politics had little to do with the return of a member for St. Albans. There was but one opinion, among all whom we examined, as to the gross and general venality existing in the borough." At the election of 1841, when the bribery oath was administered to every voter who came to the poll, there was a curious instance of compromise with conscience. A voter had received a bribe, but before taking the oath he returned the money, then took the oath, and afterwards claimed and received the money! In accordance with the report of the commissioners, an act of Parliament was passed (15th and 16th Victoria, ch. 9) for the disfranchisement of the borough. The disfranchisement was a source of satisfaction rather than of regret to the inhabitants who had kept aloof from the corrupt practices which prevailed, and even many of those who had not kept aloof from them were glad to be quit of them for ever, though at the cost of disfranchisement.

CHAPTER VII.

Modern town of St. Albans—View of it from the Verulam Hills—The situation of the Town, its topography, trade, and population—The Liberty of St. Albans—The Bishopric of St. Albans.

HAVING concluded our sketch of the history of St. Albans, we will proceed to speak of the modern city of St. Albans, and to describe, as fully as the limits of our space will allow, the places and buildings of interest that are to be found in the city and its neighbourhood. In making this survey with us, the reader will find the interest he may derive from it very much heightened by calling to mind the historic incidents and associations with which we have endeavoured to make him familiar.

The finest view of St. Albans may be obtained from the south side of the raised ground where still, in the ruins of the massive walls, may be seen the traces of the power of the Romans, the once mighty conquerors of the world, and of the extent of the city of Verulam, from which St. Alban was led forth to die, the first British martyr to the faith of Christ. From this eminence, the site of ancient Verulam, the scene is one of picturesque beauty. On the opposite hill stands the city of St. Albans; and on the spot where St. Alban was martyred rises, in massive grandeur, the venerable Abbey Church. The little river Ver, from which the ancient city took its name, meanders gracefully through the valley; and in summer time the fertile corn-fields, the green meadows, and the sylvan scenery complete a picture which is very pleasant to look upon.

The modern city of St. Albans is situated on the north-east side of the river Ver, and lies in three distinct parishes, of which the Abbey forms the centre. The north and greatest part of the east side of the city is in St. Peter's parish, and the north-west part is in St. Michael's parish.

St. Stephen's parish, which is south-west of St. Albans, includes within it but a small portion of the borough or the city proper. The principal streets are High Street, George Street, Rome Land Hill, and Fishpool Street, which run in a south-west direction to St. Michaels; Holywell Street or Hill, which runs north-east and south-west, and leads over the river Ver, to St. Stephen's Church, and in the direction of Watford; and St. Peter's Street, which is one of the widest and handsomest streets in the county, and is a continuation of Chequer Street (which begins at the top of Holywell Hill) and of the Market Place. St. Peter's Church stands at the top of the street, and near it two roads diverge, the one leading north-east to Sandridge, and the other to Luton. The Old London Road runs from Holywell Hill, and the New London Road at right angles, at the top of the hill, the two roads meeting together about a quarter of a mile from the city. Of late years the city, and especially the north-eastern part of it, lying between Bernard's Heath and the Midland Railway Station has very much increased, and is still increasing. A considerable portion of land, known as St. Peter's Park, has been planted and laid out for the erection of villas, new roads have been made, and these will form a pleasant addition to the suburbs of the city. Other estates in the same quarter have been sold for building purposes. Altogether a prosperous future appears to lie before the good city of St. Albans.

The staple trade of the city is the manufacture of straw hats, in which women are principally employed, and which therefore accounts for the considerable numerical superiority of women over men in St. Albans. The population of the extended city, according to the census of 1881, was 10,930; and since that date a considerable increase has taken place.

St. Albans was, up to the year 1875, the chief town of the Liberty of St. Alban, the ancient jurisdiction of the abbots. This liberty, which contained twenty-three parishes, and was nearly co-extensive with the Hundred of Cassio, possessed an independent legal jurisdiction, a separate commission of peace, and had its own gaol and quarter-sessions; but by the County of Hertford and

Liberty of St. Alban Act, 1874 (the 37th and 38th Vict., cap. 45), the two jurisdictions were fused, and two divisions of the county were formed, the eastern being called the Hertford division, and the western the Liberty of St. Alban division. The quarter-sessions for the trial of the prisoners for the latter division are now held at St. Albans by adjournment from Hertford, and the county business for both divisions is transacted at adjourned sessions, which are held at St. Albans and Hertford alternately.

The project of creating a See of St. Albans was entertained for many years before it was achieved. It was the most important part of a scheme for the extension of the episcopate, which was twice recommended by Convocation, and in 1875 it became at length embodied in a legislative enactment. The Bishopric of St. Alban's Act (the 38th and 39th Vic., chap. 34), which received the royal assent on the 29th of June, 1875, provided for the re-arrangement of the dioceses of London, Winchester, and Rochester, and the formation of a new diocese of St. Albans, to consist of the counties of Hertford and Essex, and of that part of the county of Kent which lies north of the river Thames ("or of such parts thereof as to Her Majesty may seem meet"), with St. Albans Abbey as its cathedral church. The Act provided for the sale, by the Ecclesiastical Commissioners, of Winchester House (the London house of the Bishop of Winchester), and the application of the proceeds as a basis for the endowment of the new bishopric, and for the sale of Danbury Palace (the episcopal residence in Essex of the Bishop of Rochester), the proceeds to be devoted to the provision of a residence for the Bishop of Rochester in Surrey, and of a residence for the Bishop of St. Albans. It was further enacted that whenever the commissioners certified that the Endowment Fund amounted to a sum producing (exclusive of the cost of the episcopal residence) a net income of not less than £2,000 a year, Her Majesty might, by an order in council, found the new bishopric. Winchester House was afterwards sold to the Government for the sum of £45,000, to provide additional accommodation for the War Office. By means of the liberal contributions of churchmen of the Diocese, the endowment fund at length reached the required amount, and in 1877 the new See was created by an order in Council. Dr. Claughton, Bishop of Rochester—with one exception the oldest diocese in England—became the first Bishop of the new See, and was entitled by the provision of the Act which anticipated his appointment to the same income and to the same rank and precedence in Parliament and elsewhere, as if he had continued to be Bishop of Rochester. The central position of St. Albans, its ample railway communications, its ecclesiastical history, and, above all, its magnificent Abbey, combined to render it well worthy of the new honour conferred upon it. The first Bishop of St Albans was enthroned in the Abbey with impressive ceremonial on the 12th of June, 1877. The inhabitants of St. Albans without distinction of class or creed joined in the popular demonstrations which accompanied this interesting event in the history of the town. The streets were lavishly decorated. Before the ceremony an imposing procession was formed at the Town Hall, in which the late Archbishop of Canterbury (Dr. Tait), several Bishops, a great number of clergy, the principal inhabitants of the county, the Mayor and Corporation, and other officials, including those of Harwich, Colchester, and Hertford took part. This procession having passed through the streets to the Abbey, the ceremony of enthronization was performed. After the ceremony a banquet was given by the Mayor (Mr. W. Cannon Smith) in celebration of this great occasion. The royal charter raising St. Albans to the rank of a city was granted on the 28th of August, 1877, and upon the 13th of the following September, the ancient town was in due form, and amid public rejoicings, proclaimed a city.

CHAPTER VIII.

St. Michael's Church—Its restoration—The Tomb of Francis Bacon—Its inscription—Gorhambury—Becomes the property of Sir Nicholas Bacon about the year 1550—He builds a new house—Queen Elizabeth's visits to Gorhambury—Lord Verulam retires to Gorhambury after his disgrace—The Grimston Family—Gorhambury House—Sopwell Nunnery—Its origin and history—The Holywell—St. Stephen's Church—The curious Brass Eagle—The Clock Tower—Traditions as to its origin—The date of the Tower—The Curfew Bell—Restoration of the Tower—The Corn Exchange—The Town Hall—St. Peter's Church—Its origin—Date of the present building—Repairs and alterations—Interior of the Church—Singular inscription—Monuments of interest.

THE object of greatest interest next to the Abbey Church is perhaps the Church of St. Michael, which lies on the south-west side of the town. St. Michael's Church was founded by Ulsinus, the sixth abbot. Matthew Paris records that it was erected by this abbot in 948. The late Sir Gilbert Scott, who made a careful survey of the church before its restoration, assigned the piers and arches of the nave, which were formerly supposed to be Saxon, to the twelfth century, to the clerestory and south chapel chiefly to the thirteenth century, and some windows and the roof of the nave, to the end of the fifteenth century. The tower he assigned to the sixteenth century.

The Church of St. Michael is built within the boundaries of the city of Verulam, and the chancel walls and other parts of the church are chiefly composed of Roman tiles, which were brought from the ancient city. Before the restoration, which took place in 1866, the church was in a deplorable state of decay; it was sadly disfigured with "tasteless patchings," and was blocked up with high family pews, in three of which were small fire-places, with fire-irons complete! These pews were demolished, and the whole aspect of the church, both internally and externally, underwent a thorough restoration to its former comeliness. The restored church contains a new south porch, a new east window, and a new window on the south side of the chancel. A small window was discovered on the east side of the north aisle, which had been blocked up for centuries. All the features of interest in the church were carefully preserved in the restoration.

Apart from the antiquity of St. Michael's Church, the illustrious name with which it must ever be associated makes it an object of the greatest interest. "For my burial, I desire it may be in St. Michael's Church, St. Albans; there was my mother buried, and it is the parish church of my mansion house of Gorhambury, and it is the only Christian Church within the walls of ancient Verulam." Such were the reasons why

"Large-browed Verulam,
The first of those who know,"

desired that St. Michael's Church should be his last resting place; and there, in obedience to his wishes, were laid the remains of

"The great deliverer, he who from the gloom
Of cloistered monks and jargon-teaching schools,
Led forth the true Philosophy, there long
Held in the magic chain of words and forms."

A recess on the northern side of the chancel is occupied with an alabaster statute of the great Master of Inductive Philosophy. Bacon is represented in his chancellor's robes, reclining in an elbow-chair. The monument was erected by Sir Thomas Meautys, his "faithful friend and secretary."

The inscription below the monument was written by Sir Henry Wotton, and the following translation of it is copied from the "Biographia Britannica:"—"Francis Bacon, Baron of Verulam, Viscount St. Albans, or by more conspicuous titles—of Science the Light; of Eloquence the Law, sat thus: Who after all natural Wisdom, and Secrets of Civil Life he had unfolded, Nature's law fulfilled—*Let Compounds be dissolved!* In the year of our Lord 1626; of his age, 66. Of such a man that the memory might remain, Thomas Meautys, living his attendant, dead his admirer, placed this monument."

Gorhambury, the seat of the Earl of Verulam, about a mile to the west of St. Michael's, derives its name from a nephew of Robert de Gorham, on whom he bestowed it. It was recovered to the Abbey by Abbot de la Mare, and was sold by the king at the dissolution of the monastery.

About the year 1550 it became the property of Nicholas Bacon, Esquire, afterwards Sir Nicholas Bacon, lord keeper of the Great Seal under Queen Elizabeth, of whom her majesty said that "Sir Nicholas's soul was well lodged in fat." Francis Bacon, who was the son of Sir Nicholas Bacon by his second wife, was not born at Gorhambury, but at York House, in the Strand. Sir Nicholas Bacon built, in 1563, a new house west of the present mansion, and nearer Pré Wood. Some ruins of it are still standing. Queen Elizabeth visited Sir Nicholas Bacon at Gorhambury on more than one occasion, and some of her state papers are dated from that place. This reception of royalty at Gorhambury must have been a rather expensive honour, for we find that the second visit of the queen, who stayed from Saturday till Wednesday, cost Sir Nicholas £576. The queen gave him her portrait as a mark of her royal favour, and this is still in existence at Gorhambury. After Bacon's disgrace and fall he retired to Gorhambury, and built a new house on another site, where he chiefly resided until his death, which took place in 1626. A characteristic incident is related by Aubrey: "This magnanimous lord chancellor had a great mind to have made Verulam a city again; and he had designed it to be built with great uniformity; but fortune denied it to him." After Bacon's death Gorhambury became the property of Sir Thomas Meautys, his private secretary, and it subsequently passed by marriage into the hands of Sir Harbottle Grimston, Bart., the ancestor of the present noble owner of Gorhambury. The Grimstons are descended from Sylvester, a Norman, who bore the standard of William the Conqueror at the Battle of Hastings.

Gorhambury House, which is a handsome stone building of the Corinthian order, was built between the years 1778 and 1785 by Viscount Grimston. The grand entrance is by a flight of steps beneath a handsome pediment, which is supported on elegant columns. The principal rooms contain a large and valuable collection of portraits of royal and eminent persons. The title of Earl of Verulam, which was first conferred on Sir Francis Bacon, was given to Lord Grimston (the father of the present earl) in 1815. The park and grounds of Gorhambury consist of about six hundred acres.

Returning to St. Albans, we next pay a visit to the ruins at Sopwell, which are about half a mile south-east of the town. Sopwell Nunnery was founded about the year 1140, by Geoffrey de Gorham, sixteenth abbot of St. Albans, and was of the Benedictine order. Two pious women, resolving to devote the rest of their lives to strict seclusion and mortification of the flesh, made themselves a dwelling-place on this spot with branches of trees. These two women were in the habit of steeping their crusts of bread in the water of a neighbouring well, and hence the place in after time was called Sopwell. Abbot Geoffrey built a house for them, and bestowed on them some possessions. He ordained that none should be admitted into the house but maidens, the number of them not to exceed thirteen. He also founded a chapel and a burial ground, in which none were to be buried except nuns. The possessions of the nunnery were afterwards increased by grants of land from Henry de Albini and Richard de Todeni. After the dissolution of the nunnery, Henry VIII. granted the site and buildings of the nunnery to Sir Richard Lee, who had previously obtained from the king the monastic buildings and lands of the Abbey of St. Albans. Newcome says that Sir Richard obtained Sopwell by means of the influence of his wife, who had great personal attractions, and who "was in no small favour with the king."

The ruins now extant are not, as is commonly supposed, those of Sopwell Nunnery, but of the house which was built on its site by Sir Richard Lee.* Many ladies of distinguished rank took the veil at this nunnery, and there is a tradition (which, however, has no historical foundation) that Henry VIII. was married to Anne Boleyn in the chapel here.

In a large meadow on the left, at the foot of Holywell Hill, is the well from which the nunnery obtained its name. The water of this well was in olden times believed to work miraculous cures, and many pilgrimages were made to it. The site of this well was formerly the lawn of a mansion called Holywell House, where the Dowager Countess Spencer lived after the death of Earl Spencer, in 1783. The mansion was pulled down forty years ago.

St. Stephen's Church, about one mile to the south-west of St. Albans, is one of the three churches founded by Abbot Ulsinus. It stands on the Roman road of Watling Street, and within half a mile of the walls of Verulam.

---

* When Sopwell House was pulled down ten circular medallions of stone, representing various Roman emperors, were taken away and placed in the wall of Salisbury Hall, in the parish of Shenley (where they may still be seen), by the Duke of St. Albans, the illegitimate son of Charles II., who rebuilt the Hall.

The church was probably rebuilt during the rule of Robert de Gorham, the eighteenth abbot, in the reign of Henry I.; but the present church (which was some years ago carefully restored) is chiefly of the date of the fifteenth century. It consists of a chapel on its south side, a nave, a small aisle, and a wooden tower and spire at its west end. There are a number of monumental inscriptions in the church, none of which are of any remarkable interest. There is also a curious brass eagle in the church, with an inscription (in old German characters) to George Creichtoun, Bishop of Dunkeld. This was found buried in the earth about the year 1750. It is supposed that it was brought from Scotland by Sir Richard Lee, at the same time that he brought the brass font which was placed in the Abbey Church, and that it was buried to prevent it from falling into the hands of Oliver Cromwell's soldiers during the great Rebellion.

We will now pay a visit to thê Clock Tower, a curious structure in the centre of the town. There is a tradition that two women of the city of Verulam wandered into the woods which covered the site of the present town of St. Albans,* and were benighted. They espied a light from the spot where they afterwards built a tower for the assistance of others who might lose their way in like manner. It was also supposed that the tower was erected as a military watch-tower for the protection of the city of Verulam; and another tradition declares that it was a part of the royal manor of Kingsbury. Clutterbuck says that it appears from original deeds preserved among the archives of the corporation that the tower was erected and appropriated to its present use between the years 1402 and 1407. Newcome supposes the tower to be the very building which Matthew Paris has described as existing in the time of Aelfric the Second, the eleventh

---

* The following rhyme accords with the tradition in regard to the wood:—

"When Verulam stood,
St. Albans was a wood;
But now Verulam's down,
St. Albans is a town.

abbot, who lived in the reign of Canute, and to have been part of the royal palace of Kingsbury, which was purchased of the king by this abbot, who demolished all of it except the tower, which stood nearer to the monastery than the other parts of the palace. This conjecture is of course erroneous. It is certain, however, that the tower was built before the year 1427. In a deed bearing the date of that year, we find that one Thomas Woldeye conveyed to one Henry Fouchere the Clock Tower and the land adjoining.* Sir Gilbert Scott was of opinion that the date of the tower is probably about the middle of the fifteenth century, or a little later. Some antiquaries suppose that it was built for its present use—as a clock tower. It is more likely that the chief object of its erection was the placing of the Curfew Bell (which is still in the tower) in a position near the centre of the town. Sir Gilbert says, "The tower seems to have been the old tower belfry somewhat equivalent to those in the old cities of Belgium. The lower story has evidently been built for a shop having two fronts. The whole is a very curious structure and unique in this country so far as my own observation extends.". The curfew bell is of about a ton weight, and has a very deep and sonorous tone, owing to the large quantity of silver in the composition of the metal. It bears the inscription—"Missi de cœlis, habeo nomen Gabrielis." The bell is now used to strike the hours of the day. The tower was for many years in a very dilapidated and unsightly condition; but it was thoroughly restored in 1865, under the direction of Sir Gilbert Scott, at a cost of £800, which had been raised by public subscription. A new clock was placed in it by the town council, and the restored tower is now an ornament to the town, as well as an interesting relic of mediæval times.

The Corn Exchange, which lies on our right as we pass up the Market-place, was erected in 1857, during the mayoralty of the late Mr. John Lewis.

The next public building we come to is the Town Hall, the foundation stone of which was laid in 1829 by Mr. John Newball Bacon, the then mayor. The Town Hall

* "Unum tenementum vocatum le clockhouse cum una vacua placea adjacante."

has a classic front, facing St. Peter's Street, with a pediment supported on columns. The building contains a large assembly room for public meetings, entertainments, &c., and a court house in which the Petty and Quarter Sessions and the County Court for the district of St. Albans are held. It also contains the Town Council Chamber and various other apartments. The old town hall was sold and converted into dwelling-houses on the erection of this building, and the greater part of it is now the premises of the *Herts Advertiser* Office. The borough police cells in Chequer Street were built in 1861.

St. Peter's Church is situated at the north end of St. Peter's Street. The church was founded in Saxon times by Abbot Ulsinus. It was originally built in the form of a Latin cross, with a tower rising from the intersection of the nave, chancel, and transept; but the church now consists of only a nave, chancel, and tower; the latter being at its east end and built up from the ground. The present building has undergone many repairs and alterations. The old tower, being in a very ruinous condition, was demolished, and in 1801 the floor of the belfry fell into the body of the church and did great damage. In 1803 an Act of Parliament was passed which appointed trustees, with the power to obtain £4,000 for the restoration of the church, by levying a rate on the parishioners. The tower and chancel were rebuilt of smaller size, and the transepts were taken down. The present tower, which is embattled, is of stuccoed brick, and its height is sixty-seven feet. In the interior of the church a light and graceful series of pointed arches are supported on clustered pillars which separate the aisles from the nave. The style of the church is, for the most part, late perpendicular. The windows of the aisles are large and elegant, and the clerestory windows are obtusely arched. There are some remains of ancient glass in the windows of the north aisle, and some modern stained glass windows, by Capronnier, of Brussels. The pulpit, which also came from the Continent, is a fine specimen of wood carving. Before its restoration in 1804, the church contained many curious monumental brasses. One of the most singular inscriptions in the church was that on a slab in the chancel, engraved in a double circle between the leaves of a rose. The outer circle read thus :—

> " Lo all that ere I spent that some time had I ;
> All that I gave in good intent that now have I ;
> That I neither gave nor lent that now abie I ;
> That I kept till I went, that lost I."

The inner circle expressed the same sentiments in Latin :—

> " Quod Expendi habui,
> Quod Donavi habeo,
> Quod Negavi punior
> Quod Servavi perdidi."

The remains of many of the soldiers slain in the battles of St. Albans were buried in St. Peter's Church and churchyard. Amongst those interred in the church were Sir Bertin Entwysel, Knight of Lancashire, and the Ralphs Babthorpe (father and son), of Babthorpe, in Yorkshire, on whom an epitaph, in Latin and English, is recorded by Weever and Chauncey. Sir Bertin Entwysel was wounded at the first battle of St. Albans, and he died on the following day, " He was beryed," says Leland, " under the plase of the Lectorium in the quyre, whereas a memorial of him ther yet remeyneth." The memorial here spoken of was the brass figure of a knight in armour. There were formerly many other inscriptions in the church, one of which was to the memory of Edmond Westby, who died in 1475. This gentleman was hundredor and bailiff of the Liberty of St. Alban ; and it is recorded that Henry VI. quartered himself in his house while the first battle of St. Albans was being fought. In the chancel there is a tablet to the memory of Dr. Rumney, who was vicar of St. Peter's for twenty-eight years, and who is referred to in Dr. Cotton's *Mirza to Selim*. He died in 1743. Against the west wall of the church is a tablet to the memory of Robert Clavering, M.B., scholar of Christ Church, Oxford, who died in 1747, aged 29. There is a Latin inscription, and beneath it some English verse, composed by Dr. Cotton, the celebrated author of " Visions in Verse," and "' The Fireside." Dr. Cotton himself, with his two wives,

Anne and Hannah, was buried in St. Peter's churchyard. Dr. Cotton was an eminent English physician and poet, and was born in 1707. He had an establishment in St. Albans for the reception of persons of unsound mind, which he called *Collegium Insanorum*. He was a very kind and amiable man, and his treatment of lunatics was most successful. The poet Cowper, who was born at Great Berkhampstead, in this county, was for a considerable time a patient of Dr. Cotton, and in one of his letters bears warm testimony to the doctor's kindliness and goodness of disposition. He writes, "I was not only treated with kindness by him while I was ill, and attended with the utmost diligence, but when my reason was restored to me, and I had so much need of a religious friend to converse with, and to whom I could open my mind on the subject without reserve, I could hardly have found a fitter person for the purpose. The doctor was as ready to administer relief to me in this article likewise, and as well qualified to do it as in that which was more immediately his province." Dr. Cotton died in August, 1788, aged 81 years. Against the west wall of the interior of the church is a bust with an inscription to the memory of Edward Strong, of New Barns, who, "equally with its ingenious architect, Sir Christopher Wren, and its truly pious diocesan, Bishop Compton, shared the felicity of seeing both the beginning and finishing of that stupendous fabric the Cathedral Church of St. Paul, about which he was employed as mason." He died in February, 1783. The tower of the church contains one of the finest peals of ten bells in the kingdom.

CHAPTER IX.

St. Albans clergymen ejected by the Act of Uniformity—Pemberton's Almshouses—Tradition as to their origin—Lord Chief Justice Pemberton—The Marlborough Buildings — Christ Church — The Dissenting Chapels—The New Gaol.

ONE of the clergymen ejected in 1662 by the Act of Uniformity was Mr. W. Haworth, vicar of St. Peter's. It is recorded in reference to Mr. Haworth that the St. Albans Abbey was desecrated by human bloodshed in the following manner:—Mr. Haworth, the ejected vicar, was specially invited to preach a funeral sermon. His old pulpit being firmly closed against him, the congregation adjourned to the cloisters of the Abbey. The soldiers appeared in the midst of the sermon and proceeded to arrest him. One of the audience interposed, and he was immediately shot dead. Mr. Haworth was tried at Hertford Assizes for the offence against the Act of Uniformity, and a penalty was imposed upon him, whilst the soldier who committed the murder escaped punishment. Mr. Haworth settled at Hertford, where he founded the Independent Church, of which he remained pastor till his death. Mr. Partridge, the ejected vicar of St. Michael's, also became the minister of a Nonconformist church.

Near the north-west side of St. Peter's Church are Pemberton's Almshouses, erected for six poor widows, in pursuance of the will of Roger Pemberton, Esq., who was Sheriff of Herts in 1620. By his will the sum of £5, issuing from his manor of Shelton, in Bedfordshire, was ordered to be appropriated to the maintenance of these poor widows for ever. There is a little court in front of the almshouses, and an arrow is stuck upright in the brickwork. Upon this arrow hangs a tale. It is said that Roger Pemberton, the founder, accidentally shot a poor woman who was a widow, and in order to make atonement for the grievous wrong he had unwittingly done, he founded these almshouses for poor widows, and placed the arrow there as a memorial of the unfortunate accident. Roger Pemberton was the grandfather of Sir Francis Pemberton, who was educated in St. Albans, and in 1681 was made Chief Justice of the Common Pleas.

The Marlborough Buildings—or "The Buildings," as they are locally termed—are the principal almshouses in St. Albans. They are situated in the Hatfield Road, not far from St. Peter's Church, and form three sides of a parallelogram. They consist of nine almshouses, each house containing four rooms, and having a detached arden. Sarah, Duchess of Marlborough, built and endowed these almshouses for the comfortable support and maintenance of thirty-six poor persons—eighteen poor men and eighteen poor women. About the year 1735 the Duchess purchased the Manor of Newland Squillers, in St. Peter's parish, and the manor house stood where the almshouses stand now. This house had been let as a boarding-school for boys of dissenting parents. The school acquired considerable reputation; and Dr. Philip Doddridge, Dr. Aikin, and other celebrated dissenting ministers, received their early education here. The Duchess of Marlborough pulled down the manor house, and built the present almshouses on the site. She generously endowed the charity, provided that she herself should have the sole management of it during her lifetime, and that after her death it should be under the direction of the Lord of the Manor of Sandridge. She also provided that £20 should be paid annually to the rector of the Abbey Church and the vicar of St. Peter's, "for overlooking the poor that shall be placed in the same almshouses." The management of the charity is now placed in the hands of Trustees. The charity is a noble one, and it is admirably administered. The inmates of the buildings are elderly men and women in reduced circumstances, who have yet some small income of their own, which, with the help of the charity, suffices for their comfortable livelihood. It affords a home for thirty-six persons, with a gift of £13 a year to each.

Another charitable institution is the Hospital and Dispensary, which is situate on Holywell Hill. The hospital is open at all times for accidents without any recommendation.

Christ Church is the only ecclesiastical edifice that remains to be described, and it is the only church in this neighbourhood of a classic style of architecture. The church, which is situated in the Verulam Road, is an excellent specimen of Italian art. Even people with strong preferences for Gothic church architecture, must, we think, confess to a liking for this little building. The interior of the church is extremely light and elegant, though we miss the grace of the pointed arch, and the noble proportions of the Gothic style. The erection of Christ Church was begun in the year 1848 by Mr. Alexander Raphael, M.P. for St. Albans, who designed it for a Roman Catholic chapel, and intended to found here an order of Sisters of Mercy, and other Catholic organizations. While, however, the works were in progress Mr. Raphael died. All further progress was then stopped, and the church remained in an unfinished state till 1856, when it was bought by the late Mrs. Worley, of New Barns, who completed the erection of the church, and munificently endowed it as a Protestant place of worship in connection with the Establishment. Mrs. Worley also erected a parsonage house adjoining the church, with which it is united by a corridor. Christ Church was made a district church for St. Michael's parish, and it was consecrated by the Bishop of Carlisle (the late Dr. Montague Villiers). April the 18th, 1859. The style of the church may be denominated Lombardo-Italian. It consists of a tower at the west end, a nave, a chancel, with a sacristry and organ-chamber on its north and south sides. The exterior is built of Bath stone, and the church is raised on a high plinth. The nave is lighted by windows of two lights, with geometrical tracery. The chancel has a triplet window on each face, is separated from the nave by an arch of two orders, and by elaborate moulded wood-work from the organ-chamber and sacristry. The arches and piers are richly decorated with conventional foliage.

We have described the churches, and now we must say a word or two about the chapels of St. Albans. The

Dissenters are a very numerous and influential body in this city, but their places of worship do not possess any features of architectural or antiquarian interest. The improved taste in regard to ecclesiastical architecture, which has made of late years almost as much progress amongst Dissenters as amongst Churchmen, has not yet been practically manifested by the dissenting communities in St. Albans. The most that can be said of any of the St. Albans chapels is that they are of a substantial and respectable appearance. The introduction of Wesleyan Methodism into St. Albans is attributed to one John Copplestone, a weaver, who was the son of a clergyman of the Church of England officiating at Luton. The present Wesleyan chapel, which is in Dagnall Street, was built in 1841. The Baptist chapel is in the same street. It is the largest Nonconformist place of worship in St. Albans, and has undergone successive alterations and improvements. The church was originally a branch of the large church at Kensworth, in this county, which was the parent of nearly half the associated Baptist churches of Herts and Beds, and appears to have been founded in the reign of Charles I. The present chapel was erected about the year 1720, "at the joint expense of the Rev. Mr. Harding and the Rev. Hugh Smith, co-pastors, Mr. Philip Smith, and Lady Harrington." It is a rather remarkable fact that a former minister of the chapel, the Rev. John Gill, who died in 1809, filled that office for fifty years, and that the Rev. William Upton, who was ordained in 1821, occupied that position for forty-four years. Mr. Upton died in 1865.

The Congregational Chapel is in Spicer-street, and is a plain brick building, with a school-room attached. The chapel was built in 1811. There is an old chapel in Dagnall-street, which was formerly a Presbyterian place of worship. The celebrated Dr. Samuel Clarke, author of "Scripture Promises," was once minister of this chapel. While Philip Doddridge was at school at St. Albans he formed an acquaintance with Dr. Clarke, and after he had made up his mind to be a dissenting minister he resided at Dr. Clarke's house, and there prepared himself, with the help of his friend and benefactor, for the sacred duties of that office Dr. Clarke was succeeded by the Rev. Joseph Hirons, who was minister of the chapel sixty years. Like many other Presbyterian Chapels it fell into the hands of the Unitarians. It is now used by the Primitive Methodists.

The St. Albans Tabernacle (Baptist) is situate in Victoria-street, and was opened for Divine worship in August, 1882.

There is a Calvinistic-Baptist chapel in the Verulam-road, and a chapel belonging to the Open Brethren in the Lattimore-road. A Quaker's meeting-house formerly stood in Dagnall-street, but there is now no place of worship in St. Albans for the Society of Friends.

A new Gaol for the Borough and Liberty of St. Alban was erected on the north-east side of the town in 1867, and is now the County Prison. The Midland Railway passes close to this building, and a view of it may also be obtained from the St. Albans and Hatfield Branch of the Great Northern Railway. The building is rather imposing in its proportions, and has not been made unnecessarily grim or ugly. It is castellated. The female prison is a separate building, and so is the governor's house. The principal feature of the prison is the complete and extensive arrangements for carrying out the separate systems of prison discipline. There are eighty-five cells in the male prison, and fourteen in the female prison, making ninety-nine in all. The chapel, which is on the north side of the building, is handsome and spacious.

GUIDE
TO
ST. ALBANS ABBEY.

GUIDE TO ST. ALBANS ABBEY.

CHAPTER X.

The Abbey Church—Its Restoration—The Abbey as seen in the distance—Its Associations—Its Form and Material—The Central Tower and Turrets—Remains of the Cloisters—The Lady Chapel—The Western Entrance—Interior of the Abbey from the Western Entrance—The Nave—Its varying styles of Architecture—Examples of Early English and Decorated Styles in Contrast—Mouldings of the Arches—Reconstruction of the Nave—The Work of John de Cella and of William de Trumpington—Destruction of Norman Piers—Decorated Work of Hugh de Eversden—The Great West Window—Ancient Piscina—Discovery of Stone Coffins—The Roof—Sir John Mandeville—Alexander Neckham—Series of Frescoes on the Norman Piers—The Chapel of St. Andrew—The Forensic Parlour—St. Cuthbert's or the Rood Screen—Dedication of the Altars—The Organ.

WE now turn our attention to that building which is at once the pride and glory of St. Albans—its ABBEY CHURCH. In looking upon it, we know not what to admire most—the grandeur of its design, the magnitude and dignity of its proportions, the beauty of its architectural details, or its venerable antiquity.

Before, however, entering upon a description of the Abbey, it may be convenient in this place to say something about the extensive restorations it has undergone. Before the work of restoration was begun many parts of the Abbey were in a very decayed and ruinous state, and it was evident that a great deal more was necessary in order to stay the ruthless hand of Time than could be accomplished by means of merely local subscriptions. Since the dissolution of the monastery various repairs and restorations have been made from time to time. In the reign of James the First, two thousand pounds were collected under royal authority and expended in the restoration of the church. Subscriptions were also collected by royal briefs in 1681, 1721, and 1764, besides a grant out of certain ecclesiastical funds in 1689. In February, 1832, a part of the wall of the upper parapet on the south-west side of the Abbey fell upon the roof in two huge masses, and so great was the concussion that a large portion of the massive roof was driven into the aisle below. Great damage was thus occasioned, and a voluntary collection was made for the repair of the church, which was chiefly confined, however, to the county of Hertford. The present work of restoration may be said to have been initiated by a former rector, the Rev. Dr. Nicholson, whose love and veneration for the Abbey, and zealous efforts to rescue it from decay and destruction, ought not to be forgotten. In 1856 a county meeting was held at St. Albans to consider the best means of restoring and upholding the Abbey Church, and of obtaining for it the dignity of a cathedral. The Government of the day, however, held out no hope of the creation of a See of St. Albans. The subscription list was cancelled, and another opened. With the amount of the second subscription the committee purchased a plot of ground on the north side of the Abbey, in order to prevent some cottages being built upon it. In 1860 and 1861, some important works were carried out by Mr. G. G. Scott (afterwards Sir Gilbert Scott), the late eminent architect and church restorer. In August, 1870, the great tower of the Abbey was found by Mr. Chapple, Sir Gilbert Scott's able clerk of the works, to be in a most dangerous condition. The two eastern piers showed signs both of subsidence and of actual crushing, and it was evident that the tower was sinking. Happily, the danger was discovered in time, and effectual measures were at once taken to avert such a catastrophe as the fall of the tower, and the consequent destruction of the church. Owing to its stupendous size and weight, the work of shoring the tower was one of no small difficulty, but it was successfully accomplished. This was followed by the restitution to the piers of large portions which had long ago been cut away from them, and the piers themselves were strengthened by the substitution of sound for disintegrated material. It was discovered that a large excavation had been made in the south-eastern pier, beneath the floor, probably at the time of the Commonwealth, with a view no doubt to the destruction of the tower. The Abbey Reparation Committee was soon afterwards formed, and in April, 1871, Sir Gilbert Scott addressed a report to the chairman of the committee (the Earl of Verulam), in which he estimated that "a sum of at least £26,000 will be required for immediate and absolutely necessary structural repairs, while a further sum of £20,000 is necessary for the proper reparation of the Abbey, exclusive of any internal fittings or restorations." On the 22nd of June in the same year a very influential meeting was held at Willis's Rooms, under the presidency of Lord Verulam, and eloquent appeals were made on behalf of the Reparation Fund by the late Bishop Wilberforce, the late Dean Stanley, the Marquis of Salisbury, the late Earl Stanhope, and others, who urged that the work of preserving St. Albans Abbey ought to be regarded as a national undertaking.

Some time afterwards, the Marchioness of Salisbury, the late Countess of Essex, the Countess of Verulam, and the Countess Cowper formed a committee of ladies, in order to obtain means for the rescue of the lady chapel from the ruin and desolation which had overtaken it, and a special report upon its history, condition, and the required restorations was presented by Sir Gilbert Scott to Lady Salisbury.

The restoration of the Abbey has proceeded by rather slow degrees, but yet with as much expedition as the nature of the work and the funds placed from time to time at the disposal of the committee will allow. Sir Gilbert Scott took the most scrupulous care to preserve or reproduce every ancient feature, however minute or apparently insignificant. The objects he religiously set before him were to " retain every fragment remaining of ancient work, to obliterate not one scrap of ancient wrought surface, to insert no new stone which is not essential, and so far as possible to repair the ancient structure without in any degree infringing on its antiquity." We shall describe hereafter the details of the restoration, and the discoveries which have been made during its progress. Mr. Miskin, of St. Albans, has been the contractor employed for the greater part of the work. Not only was the tower made perfectly safe, but it was stripped of its external plaster, so as to expose to view the Roman tiles of which it is composed. The whole fabric of the eastern portion of the church, including the choir, presbytery, transepts, aisles, and saint's chapel, has been strengthened and restored. The restoration of the lady chapel and the ante-chapel has also been carried out as far as the funds subscribed for this purpose permit. When part of the south side of the nave (the clerestory and triforium) which for some time had been inclining more and more outwards, was found to be in actual danger of falling, Sir Edmund Beckett generously came to the rescue (the Reparation Committee having no funds for this purpose), and the work of shoring it was quickly carried out. In 1876 the Reparation Committee was reconstituted; a new faculty for repairs was obtained, and a contract entered into with Messrs. Longmire and Burge. The old low-pitched roof of the nave was raised clear of the walls by means of screw power, and the five south bays were successfully restored, chiefly by means of hydraulic power, to their original vertical position—a perilous and difficult undertaking. The roof was then replaced, and the arcade strengthened by means of flying buttresses and groining. Sir Gilbert Scott died in March, 1878, leaving incomplete the great work to which he had devoted himself with singular ardour and enthusiasm. His method of restoration at St. Albans, as elsewhere, has been subjected to hostile criticism, but the strongest opponents of "conjectural restoration" must, if they are candid, admit that his work was always conservative in intention if not always in result. No man ever had a profounder admiration of the genius and skill of the old church builders, and the charge sometimes brought against him of spoiling the work he had taken infinite pains to preserve must have stung him to the quick. A great controversy was occasioned after Sir Gilbert Scott's death by a proposal to substitute for the flat roof of the nave, which was very much out of repair, and was said to date only from the latter half of the 15th century, a roof "of the original pitch indicated by the weathering on the tower." Sir Gilbert had intended, if possible, to restore the roof to its original high pitch. The opponents of the change objected that the new roof would dwarf the tower. They also contended that the western part of the roof was reconstructed of a low pitch after the recorded fall of a portion of it in the year 1323, and that the remainder was reconstructed early in the 15th century. Mr. Street, however, assigned the western part of the roof to the close of the century. The "battle of the roofs," after being fiercely fought, ended, as the visitor will see for himself, in the victory of "high pitch" over "low pitch," and also in one or two unfortunate secessions from the Faculty Committee. In the year 1880 the west front of the Abbey, having threatened a state of collapse, Sir Edmund Beckett obtained, though not without opposition, a faculty for rebuilding it at his own expense and in accordance with his own design. This work he undertook and completed at a cost to himself of more than £20,000. The apex stone of the great cross on the new front was fixed on July 25, 1883, by Sir Edmund. The cross is more than a ton in weight, and its extreme height from the floor of the great porch is 109 feet 2½ inches.

The exterior of the Abbey, when seen in the distance, is imposing in its stately yet simple grandeur. And if the visitor knows its history, and can call to mind as in a moving panorama the scenes with which it is associated —the death of the first British martyr, who shed his blood on that spot ; the long line of abbots who have ruled there in princely state ; the Benedictine monks who, in sombre garb, trod its hallowed ground ; the kings and queens who held it high honour to be allowed to worship there ; the weary pilgrims to the shrine of St. Alban joyfully hailing the first glimpse of its massive battlements ; and the monkish processions, the daily watch, the nightly vigil, the solemn rites, the gorgeous ceremonies of olden times : as these all pass before his mental vision—how varied his emotions, how absorbing his interest !

The Abbey Church of St. Albans is in the form of a Latin cross, and consists of a central tower, nave, choir, two transepts, presbytery, and lady chapel. The materials of which a considerable portion is built are far older than the church itself. The central parts of the church (which are the most ancient) are built of Roman tiles, obtained from the ruins of the city of Verulam, It must be confessed that in the close inspection of the exterior the general effect is a little marred by this rude admixture of Roman tiles with other materials. The height of the central tower (which, with the transepts, one bay of the aisles of the choir, and a large portion of the nave, was the work of Abbot Paul de Caen, the first Norman abbot—1066-77) is 144 feet. The battlements are of later date than the lower portions of the tower, which is divided by bands into three stages, on each side of which are two double rows of windows having semi-circular arches beneath a like arch of larger size. The Saxon baluster columns in the triforium are probably portions of the very church erected by King Offa. The spandrel beneath the smaller, and above the large and smaller arches, is perforated with diamond-shaped apertures for the purpose of giving vent to the sound of the bells. In the lower stage are eight circular windows, which admit light into the belfry. The tower terminates in circular turrets at the four angles.* The east end of the choir and the extremities of the transepts are terminated by turrets rising above the roof and embattled. The turrets at the western angles of the transepts are of the Norman era. On the south side of the nave are the remains of eight blind arches. These formed the side of the cloisters, which were 150 feet square.

The lady chapel and ante-chapel are situate at the east end of the church—and though one of the least ancient and most elaborately beautiful portions of the whole building, were, until the recent restorations, in an extremely ruinous condition, while retaining traces of their former elegance and grace. The lady chapel, with the ante-chapel

* The tower was formerly surmounted by a short leaden spire, which was removed because it was considered out of character with the architecture of the church. It was, however, a distinctive Hertfordshire feature.

or eastern aisle, communicated with the church by five pointed arches, but became separated from the main body of the building as a consequence of Edward the Sixth's charter empowering the mayor and burgesses to erect a grammar school in the church. The arches connecting the ante-chapel and the lady chapel with the church were blocked up in 1553, and a public thoroughfare constructed. During the progress of the restoration, the arches have been opened; and the public footway now runs round the ante-chapel instead of through it. The lady chapel itself, used for more than three centuries as a schoolroom, has been restored to the church.

At the west end of the church is the grand entrance. As this part of the Abbey has been almost entirely rebuilt by Sir Edmund Beckett, the following description of it as it existed before the rebuilding, given in former editions of this work, may be of interest:—

"There is a large projecting porch, supported on massive buttresses, and ornamented by mouldings, the outermost of which rests on two carved human heads, which are decayed. The porch opens by a high pointed arch, above which are shields, bearing the arms (three crowns) of Offa (founder of the monastery) and the arms of the Abbey, which are now the borough arms. Pointed and trefoil arches adorn the interior of the porch, and these are sustained on clustered pillars of Purbeck marble, with carved capitals, which are much defaced. There are three clustered pillars in the centre, with a pointed arched doorway on each side, and three pointed arches above. The doors are of finely-carved oak. Over the entrance is the great west window."

Abbot John de Cella (1185 to 1214) conceived the idea of pulling down the Norman west front and rebuilding it in the First Pointed or Early English style of his own period. Two western towers and three porches were included in his design, which, however, was never carried out in its integrity. The three portals were built, the great central porch and a porch to each of the aisles. During some repairs to this part of the Abbey, early in the eighteenth century, the aisle porches were mutilated and blocked up from the outside with their own fragments, and the west front was disfigured in other ways. At the time Sir Edmund Beckett obtained his Faculty the front was in a dangerous as well as in a dilapidated and unsightly condition. Sir Edmund's design included the reopening and repair of these beautiful porches of Abbot John de Cella, and the substitution of a decorated for the old decayed perpendicular window; the excavation of the porch floors to their ancient levels, and the construction of a flight of five steps to reach the ancient level of the nave floor. Messrs. Buckler, who discovered the original level, were of opinion that the steps were never made, but Mr. Chapple says he has "discovered pavement well worn with the feet at the lower level," from which he concludes that the general floor of the nave must have been at one time approached by steps. Ancaster stone is the material used in the rebuilding of this part of the Abbey. We may here mention that Sir Edmund Beckett has resolved upon the thorough repair of the stonework of the Decorated period on the south side (about 98 feet in length) and of the Norman and Decorated windows; the repair of the exterior of the Norman choir; the covering of the aisles of the nave with high pitched roofs, corresponding in outline to those now covering the Early English portion westward; and the erection of new buttresses for the support of the cloister wall. When the restoration of this part of the Abbey has been completed, it is intended to put a high pitched roof on the north transept, and to insert a new north window.

The external length of the church from east to west is 549 feet 6 inches, and it is therefore the longest church in England. The aisles are 276 feet long and 65 feet broad, the central tower is 40 feet square and 144 feet high, the two transepts are 189 feet long, the choir with side aisles 175 feet by 65 feet. The distance between the high altar and St. Cuthbert's or the roodscreen is 175 feet. *

* Most of these measurements were taken by Mr. John Harris, architect, to whom we are also indebted for the following statistics of the comparative length of the longest churches in England:— Winchester, 545 feet; Ely, 517 feet; Canterbury, 514 feet; Westminster, 511 feet 6 inches; York, 486 feet; St. Paul's, 460 feet; Lincoln, 460 feet. St. Albans Abbey, therefore, is clearly entitled to the pre-eminence of being known as the longest ecclesiastical edifice in England.

Judging only from the exterior of the building, which is remarkable for its simplicity and plainness, a stranger would have but little conception of its internal magnificence, and of its variety, elegance, and richness of detail. The Abbey is a museum of ecclesiastical architecture, a perpetual and inexhaustible study. The striking diversity in the styles, though destroying unity and harmony of design, is itself of the greatest value to the art student. "In St. Albans Abbey," says a learned antiquary, "the style of every age may be traced in its progression, from the time of the Normans to the reign of Edward the Fourth." "The Abbey of St. Albans," says another writer, "may be considered as a vast museum, or school of arts, where the student may improve and perfect his designs upon the best models, and which, were every other lost, might still supply the elements for constructing a masterpiece of ecclesiastical architecture."

Having viewed the exterior of the Abbey, we will now proceed to an examination of the interior, beginning at the west end of the nave. No-one can fail to admire the grandeur of design and elaborate workmanship of this part of the church; but what interests us even above these are the examples it gives us of three grand periods of church architecture—the Norman, or Romanesque, style of the 11th century, the Early English, or First Pointed, style of the 13th century, and the Decorated, or Second Pointed, style of the 14th century. The place on the north series of arches where the Norman ends and the Pointed begins deserves our notice. The clustered Early English pillars of the sixth arch of the nave spring out of the massive Norman pier, and the window of the clerestory above this arch is Early Pointed, though there is but one window instead of two in the bay. Standing against the western part of the Abbey, and looking over St. Cuthbert's screen (as it is incorrectly called) and the altar screen, to the window of the saint's chapel—the entire length of the church—we are equally impressed with the beauty and grandeur of the scene before us. Here we may mark the successive architectural changes which have been made in the building. The six massive Norman piers on the north side belong to the original structure of Abbot Paul. To these succeeds the Early English work of Abbot Trumpington. The first three arches of each tier on the south side of the nave are very much like those on the north, but the column which supports the fifth great arch is larger than any of the others, and is flat on its north and south sides. Here it is we see in juxtaposition the Early English and Decorated styles. The latter has greater variety and beauty of moulding than the former. The elegance and richness of these arches of the Decorated period are a constant theme of admiration, and the student may study with profit the distinctive features of the two periods—the one of the 13th and the other of the 14th century. The outer mouldings of the Decorated arches terminate in stone carvings of human heads, which are sculptured in bold relief. The first of these (the sixth column from the west end) represents an abbot, with a shield above charged with *fleur de lis* ; the second a king, above which are the arms of Mercia (the three crowns) ; the third a queen, with three lions passant ; and the fourth a bishop, with a shield charged with a cross between five martlets (the arms of Edward the Confessor and of Westminster).*

The first great structural alteration in the original Norman church was, as we have said, begun by John de Cella. This abbot, who governed the monastery for nearly twenty years, was a man of great learning and of great artistic taste and skill, but unfortunately he had no business capacity. He demolished the vast Norman façade, and forgetful, writes Matthew Paris, of the admonition mentioned in the Gospel to him who is about to build, to compute the cost, lest " all begin to jest at him, saying, ' This man began to build and was not able to finish,' laid the foundation of the new work, without having the means of carrying it on." He appears to have been victimised by his first builder, Hugh Goldcliff, " a man deceitful and false, but an excellent workman," and after employing three successive architects, and exhausting all methods of obtaining money, he was obliged to limit himself to the erection of the three beautiful portals in the western front

---

* The sculptured heads are believed to represent the Abbot Paul, King Offa, and Editha, Queen of Edward the Confessor.

with their exquisite marble columns and carved capitals. " I doubt," wrote Sir Gilbert Scott, " whether there exists in England a work so perfect in art, as the half-ruined portals of St. Albans. I venerate the architect who designed them, who, I believe, was Abbot John de Cella's second architect, Gilbert de Eversholt. His work is contemporary with two others, which are as fine as almost any in existence—the western porch at Ely, and the choir of St. Hugh at Lincoln. All of these were the works of the earliest perfected Early English, after it had thrown off the square form of the Romanesque capital." At the death of John de Cella, his successor, William de Trumpington (1214—1235) resumed the work of rebuilding, which de Cella had been forced to relinquish. Trumpington, being a man of business, modified in a remorseless manner—for the sake of economy—the designs of his predecessor. This was seen by examining the works of the two abbots at their points of junction. " Columns with bases for eight shafts reduced at the capitals to four ; the marble bandings prepared for the larger number, but roughly altered to suit their reduction, while the marble largely used or contemplated by the one is almost wholly omitted by the other." * By thus curtailing the designs of John de Cella, Abbot William de Trumpington was enabled not only to complete the west front, but also five bays at the west end of the nave on the south side, and four on the north, besides other works of minor importance. Abbot Trumpington's work is a very fine example of Early English ; but, to make use of an expression of Sir Gilbert Scott, it is less *spirituel* than that of his predecessor. If the illustration be not too fanciful, it may be said that the designs of de Cella compared with those of Trumpington are like the compositions of Mendelssohn compared with those of Handel. We now proceed to examine the five bays on the south side of the nave, which continued the work of Trumpington, and which form a very beautiful example of the Decorated style. During the abbacy of Hugh de Eversden (1308—1326), the Norman piers on this side of the church suddenly gave way. Wal-

---

* Sir Gilbert Scott's report.

singham has left the following account of the incident, which happened on the day of St. Paulinus, in the year 1323:—" After the celebration of the mass of the Blessed Virgin, an accident occurred of so horrible a kind that no earlier misfortune could be compared with it. For when a great multitude of men and women were gathered together in the church, praying and listening to the mass, on a sudden two immense columns on the south side of the building, as if broken off at their foundations, fell one after another with a horrible crash and ruin to the earth; and while the great crowd, both of monks and laymen, struck dumb by the disaster, were collected to gaze upon the ruin, scarcely an hour had passed when, behold! the entire wooden roof built above the columns, with the arched beams, a part of the southern aisle, as well as nearly the whole of the adjoining cloister, fell likewise to the earth." Abbot Hugh began the reconstruction of this part of the nave in the style of his own time—marked principally by the difference of the mouldings, and the substitution of the ball-flower for the dog-tooth ornament—but so far modified as to bring it as much as might be into general harmony with the older and simpler work of Abbot Trumpington. "But the difference of age cannot be mistaken; it is seen in the greater simplicity and undercutting of the mouldings of the earlier style, and in the matchless ornament of the dog-tooth standing in juxtaposition with the ball-flower and roset. These are introduced sparingly; and, as if imitation in the present instance were indispensable, the same proportion and situation are assigned to the later ornament as to the former." * In the lady chapel, which was also for the most part the work of Hugh Eversden, we find the same style of architecture carried out without restraint, and with more lavish profusion of ornament.

Above the west entrance to the church is the great west window that Sir Edmund Beckett has substituted for the Perpendicular window supposed to have been the work of Abbot Wheathamstead.

* Buckler's "St. Albans Abbey."

At the west end of the north aisle is an elegant Stoup of which we give an engraving. In the north aisle there

STOUP.

are three stone coffins, which were discovered some years ago below the pavement. On the lid of one of the coffins being raised a perfect skeleton was found, clothed in a woollen garb, which makes it probable that these were the remains of a Benedictine monk. Pieces of hazel wood (the remains of an hazel wand) were found in the coffin, which may now be seen in the saint's chapel.

Under the west window is a Latin inscription recording that the supreme courts of justice were twice held in the Abbey whilst the plague was raging in the metropolis— once in the reign of Henry VIII., and again in the reign of Elizabeth.

The nave ceiling is of English oak, panelled as in the fifteenth century. Not a trace of the ribs of the old panelling remained on the surface, but many pieces were found used in ceiling joists, thus showing that about the year 1683, when the Abbey underwent extensive repair, the original painted ceiling was removed, and the materials were used in another form and were repainted. The old roof was also repaired under John Mylne, architect, in 1767, and the specifications of the work are now in Mr. Chapple's possession. At the same time it was decided to remove the Norman turret in the south transept, but the Reparation Committee of that day hastily met and rescinded the resolution. A gangway is provided throughout the entire length of the new roof, communicating by a door with the tower triforium.

Above the four Early English arches on the north side is a range of eight pointed arches, each being subdivided into two smaller arches, and above these is a third range of pointed arches extending to the roof. On the second pillar from the western entrance on the north side is an inscription to the memory of Sir John Mandeville, the celebrated traveller, who was a native of St. Albans and who was supposed to have been buried here. It is affirmed however by Weever, in his "Funeral Monuments," that he saw the tomb and epitaph of Sir John Mandeville in a church in the city of Liège. Sir John was born in the town about the beginning of the fourteenth century, and wrote an account of his travels, which he published in English, French, and Latin. His writings have been compared with those of Herodotus, the father of history, but they are full of the most prodigious superstitions and falsehoods, and are chiefly valuable as showing the state of the English language in the fourteenth century. Another celebrated native of St. Albans — Alexander Neckham, or Nequam, who was known as the "Miraculum Ingenii"—is also recorded to have been buried here.

In 1862 a very remarkable series of ancient frescoes, on the western faces of the Norman piers, were brought to light by Dr. Nicholson. Each fresco has a representation of the Crucifixion (our Saviour being depicted in a bending attitude), with one of the "Glories of the Blessed Virgin" below it. Mr. J. G. Waller states that the only instance in this country in which this repetition of the subject is followed occurs on the piers of the little village church of Ulcombe, in Kent. In the earliest examples the cross takes the literal form of a tree with knots and branches. On the southern face of the most western Norman pier is a gigantic representation (much defaced) of St. Christopher holding the infant Saviour on his arm. On the sixth pier are the remains of a large figure of Christ in His glory; and on the south side of the nave are also some slight remains of frescoes in outline. The paintings of the Crucifixion have been supposed to indicate the position of altars which formerly stood beneath them, but Mr. J. G. Waller's opinion that they indicated Stations of the Cross is probably the correct one. One of the frescoes, that of an archbishop, has been conjectured to be a representation of St. Thomas à Becket. The frescoes are believed to date from the thirteenth and fourteenth centuries. The coloured patterns on the Norman arches are also assigned to the fourteenth century.

In the upper part of the second Norman pier from the screen is a staircase, which now leads from the clerestory to the roof of the north aisle.

At the west end of the north aisle may be seen the site of arches leading into the chapel of St. Andrew, part of the foundations of which still remain. This chapel contained three altars, one dedicated to St. Nicholas. An arch on the south side led to an apartment of the abbot's house, called the Forensic Parlour (with abbot's chapel over), where the guests of the monastery were first received.

In the south aisle there hangs the framework of a chaplet, and the tradition has been handed down that this was the marriage garland of a bride who died on her wedding-day, and was buried near this spot.

During the seven years (1870-77) that the work of restoration was being carried on in the other parts of the Abbey the services were held in the nave.

St. Cuthbert's, or the rood screen, which separates the nave from the choir, and originally divided the church of the monks from the church of the laity, is a good specimen of Decorated work, and dates from the middle of the fourteenth century. Richard de Albini, the fifteenth abbot, built a chapel in honour of St. Cuthbert, as an act of gratitude, it was said, for the miraculous cure of a withered arm from contact with the body of the saint at Durham.

This chapel, which was restored and enlarged by William de Trumpington, was believed to have stood eastward of the present screen, and an altar at the screen was said to be the altar of St. Cuthbert. It is clear, however, from the records of the Abbey. that the chapel was an external building " near the cloister of St. Alban." In the middle of the rood screen was an altar dedicated to the Holy Cross and to St. Amphibalus. There were three other altars, dedicated to St. Mary, all Apostles, Confessors, and St. Benedict; St. Thomas the Martyr; and St. Oswin. On the western face of the screen are traces of two altars, of a reredos, and the remains of a piscina. The diversified foliage, the richly-sculptured canopies, and the delicate mouldings of this screen well repay a careful examination. The two doorways, one on each side of the altar of the Holy Cross, were used for the passage of processions. It is intended to add new wings to the screen across the north and south aisles, and to insert a doorway in each wing, the existing doors being priests' doors only.

The great organ, which stands near St. Cuthbert's screen. is an instrument of great power and compass, and was built in 1861 at a cost of £1,200.

CHAPTER XI.

The Choir—The Font—The Choir Ceiling—Discovery of the original Paintings—South Aisle of Baptistery—Memorial Windows—Tomb and Piscina—Roger and Sigar—The Abbot's Door—Apsidal Chapels—The Slype—The Tower—Saxon Columns—The Presbytery—The Wallingford Screen—The Altar-steps and Pavement—Restorations—Tomb of Abbot Ramryge — Tomb of Abbot Wheathamstead — Monumental Brasses and Inscriptions—The New Pulpit—North Aisle of Presbytery —North Transept—The Transept Windows—Ascent to the Tower—The Belfry.

WE now pass through St. Cuthbert's screen into the choir, where we find that the great work of restoration has been accomplished. Opinions may differ as to particular details of the work, but there can be no doubt that on the whole it has been carried out in a conservative spirit.

A remarkable discovery was made during the repair of the roofs. In restoring the choir ceiling, under the paintings of the seventeenth century much older paintings were found, of which the latter were but rude imitations. The removal of the comparatively modern surface of paint was very skilfully performed, the result being the rescue from oblivion of some magnificent specimens of mediæval painting. There are sixty-six panels in eleven rows of six panels each. In each row are three panels, each charged with a shield supported by an angel alternating with a like number bearing the sacred monogram "I H C," surrounded by a scroll, with the exception of two central panels, in the sixth row, which contain representations of our Lord and the Virgin Mary. On the panels bearing shields are inserted invocations to the Trinity, and the greater part of the *Te Deum* in Latin. On the other thirty-two shields are the arms of a number of kings, princes, and saints. Among these are the shields of St. Edward, St. Alban, St. Oswin, St. George, the Kings of England, France, Spain, Portugal, Denmark, Hungary, Navarre, the Isle of Man, &c. There are also the "Shield of Faith" and the "Shield of Salvation." The bosses at the intersection of the main ribs are elaborately carved and gilt. Mr. Ridgway Lloyd, in an elaborate paper upon these paintings, which he read before the St. Albans Architectural and Archæological Society, attributes their main features to a period between 1368 and 1376; others suppose them to be the work of Abbot Wheathamstead (*circa* 1440). In removing the whitewash from the choir walls, four colossal figures in fresco were discovered at the clerestory stage, three on the north, and one on the south wall. A painting of the Trinity was also found on a pier on the north side. The new stalls erected westward of the choir are only an instalment of those which it is intended to place there. They are of the Decorated order, and as funds come in it is intended to continue them on the north and south sides, as far as the tower piers. The stalls already fixed are in memory of the late Archdeacon Mildmay. The central doorway has been erected by the Bishop of St. Albans to the memory of his son-in-law, Captain Ronald Campbell, of the Coldstream Guards, who was killed in the Zulu War. On the doorway is a beautifully carved figure of St. Alban. The Bishop's throne is a temporary erection borrowed from Rochester Cathedral.

Entering the south aisle of the choir we notice a memorial window, which is a copy of the fresco in the north transept, representing the incredulity of St. Thomas. By its side is another window, which is the gift of Messrs. Heaton and Butler, illustrating the "Baptism of our Lord," and its antitype, the "Passage of the Red Sea." The arms of Dr. Nicholson and of the borough of St. Albans are introduced into the border. Against an arched recess in the wall, which is supposed by Messrs. Buckler to be a tomb of the date of Henry the Third, is an ancient piscina, which Gough says "was removed hither from the south-west pillar of the choir when the stairs of the gallery (now demolished) were built." Above the arch there is a Latin inscription to the memory of Roger and Sigar. Sigar was a hermit, who had a cell at Northaw, of whom it was said that "being interrupted in his devotions by the nightingales and other singing birds, he drove them away by his prayers, so that they durst not sing within a mile of his cell." Roger and Sigar are supposed to have lived in the time of Geoffrey de Gorham, the sixteenth abbot. A few feet east of the piscina is the elegant arched stone doorway, probably called the Abbot's Door, it having been the main entrance from the great cloister into the church. The door is of oak, richly carved, and adorned with crockets and pinnacles

From the south aisle we pass into the south transept. In this part of the building there were formerly several apsidal chapels, which were destroyed in the time of Edward the Second. The conventual buildings were attached to this part of the church, and the entrances to them may still be seen in the southern staircase. Running parallel to the transept, and opening into it by a flight of modern steps, is a short passage, called the slype, which communicated with the cloisters and cemetery of the monks, and divided the south transept from the chapter-house On each side of the slype is a range of intersecting semi-circular arches, with capitals elaborately carved, the only example of the later Norman work to be found in the church. Sir Gilbert Scott, in reference to this slype, says—"One fragment only remains of a richer form of Norman architecture; a small chamber against the end of the south transept, which separated the chapter-house from the church. This contains details of exquisite beauty." It is conjectured that St. Cuthbert's chapel was of a similar style of architecture; and the discovery, in the course of restoration, of richly-carved capitals resembling those in the slype, affords some confirmation of the theory. Some of the carvings on the capitals of the slype represent a human mask with stems of leaves issuing from its mouth; others the heads of entwined snakes; and another, three very grotesque figures—a trio of Bacchantes.* Two blocked windows of Abbot Trumpington in this transept, and several niches, have been re-opened and restored. We now pass under the tower, which is supported on four semi-circular arches resting on massive piers. This part of the building, with the transepts, is a portion of the original Norman church, built by Abbot Paul in the last quarter of the eleventh century, soon after the introduction of the Norman style into England; and its grand simplicity presents a striking contrast to the ornate styles of the Early English and Decorated periods. Many of the columns of the triforium in the transepts and tower are Saxon baluster columns, to which Norman bases and capitals have been added; and these in all probability are remnants of the Saxon church, which was superseded by the present structure. The edges of the Roman tiles forming the materials of the arches in the triforium are now exposed to view. Over the east arch of the tower is the coat of arms of the monastery, and the roses of York and Lancaster are noticeable on the painted ceiling. From his present standpoint under the tower the visitor cannot fail to be impressed by the grandeur and beauty of the presbytery (the space between the altar-screen and the tower), with its beautiful carving, its rich tracery, and its noble monuments. The reconstruction of the eastern portion of the church was begun in the reign of Henry III.

* There are carvings of figures something like these on the capitals of the chancel-arch in the parish church of Hemel Hempstead, about seven miles from St. Albans.

(1256)—the Early English period—by John of Hertford, the twenty-third abbot, and was completed by his successors. "Nothing," writes Sir Gilbert Scott, "can be finer than the works carried out at this period. They were never perfected according to their original design; but what was done was as perfect in art as anything which its age produced." The general style of architecture in the presbytery may be said to be Early or Geometrical Decorated. The ceiling is decorated with the emblems of the lamb and the eagle—the device adopted by Abbot Wheathamstead—and illuminated with gold. It has been carefully cleansed from all modern additions, and the decorations of Abbot Wheathamstead have been restored to their pristine beauty.

The Altar, or Wallingford Screen, as it is often called, is one of the most beautiful and interesting features of the Abbey Church. This screen divides the presbytery from the saint's chapel, and was probably intended to conceal the shrine of St. Alban from the public gaze. It was erected by William Wallingford, the thirty-sixth abbot; but the arms of Wheathamstead, which are over the doors, render it probable that it was designed by that abbot, who possessed in so eminent a degree architectural knowledge and genius. The screen is one of the very best specimens of carving in stone extant, and for excellence of design and workmanship in some respects surpasses the screen of Winchester Cathedral, to which it bears a marked likeness. It is, too, one of the finest examples of the Perpendicular style of the fifteenth century. The front of it consists of three divisions—a centre and two wings. In the central part which is defaced and mutilated, may be seen the form of a cross. There is no doubt that a crucifix formerly occupied this portion of the screen,* which was formerly covered over with carved work of the last century of a very inappropriate character. Under the cross are thirteen niches, which were designed to receive images of the twelve apostles, with our Saviour in the centre. Above the door leading into the presbytery on the south side are

---

* In Dr. Stukeley's *Itiniarium Curiosum* (published in 1721), there is an engraving of the screen with this crucifix in the centre.

the ancient arms of France and England, supported by angels; and over the door on the north side are the arms of John of Wheathamstead. The altar is approached by four Purbeck marble steps, which have been substituted during the restoration for a flight of stone steps. The original steps were of Purbeck marble, and the ends of them adjoining the tomb of Abbot Ramryge were preserved. There is also a flight of five steps of polished marble leading from the eastern arch to the presbytery. A beautiful pavement of Purbeck marble (all ancient slabs repolished) has been laid in the sacrarium before the altar-screen. The floors in the choir, presbytery, and aisles have been restored to their original levels, and while this was being done the foundations of the choir stalls were discovered. All the old tile paving has been renewed, and in every instance the patterns of ancient tiles have been copied. Some of the finest examples of ancient tiles in England are here to be found, and every fragment has been preserved, and laid in the floor of the north transept. It having been found that the tower arches bore traces of decoration, the patterns have been renewed. Two ancient doorways in the presbytery have been restored, after having been blocked up for two centuries and a half. Some years ago the fragments of some beautiful tabernacle work were found by Sir Gilbert Scott behind the panelling in the south wall. This was restored, and placed over the south doorway. A similar tabernacle was erected over the north doorway, but the original pinnacles and a finial of this structure were subsequently found, and as they differed materially in detail from those on the opposite walls, the new pinnacles and finial were taken away, and the old ones substituted for them. This may be taken as a typical instance of the conservative character of the restoration.

We now turn to the beautiful chantry tomb of Abbot Ramryge (1492—1521), which occupies the lower part of a large pointed arch on the north side of the presbytery, adjoining the altar-screen. The tomb is of elaborate workmanship. Beneath its windows are rows of heraldic devices. The stone-carving of the roof of this chamber is of a very exquisite and delicate character. A curious inscription is carved in stone on the north and south sides of the exterior of the tomb : "Sancti Spiritus assit nobis gracia. Veni Sancte Spiritus, reple tuorum corda fidelium ; et tui amoris in eis ignem accende. Amen." Great care was necessary to preserve this chantry, as it had been injured and even threatened with destruction by the lateral pressure from the tower. The original incised slab of the abbot's tomb, which had been broken and removed to the south aisle of the presbytery, in order to allow of the interment of a family who had appropriated the chantry (the Ffarington family of Lancashire), has been refixed in its former place.

In the arch opposite the splendid tomb of Abbot Ramryge is the simple though elegant monument which has hitherto been assigned to Abbot Wheathamstead (1420—1464). The following is the inscription on the wall above the monument—on its south side :—

"JOHANNES—De Loco frumentario,
Quis Jacet hic ? Pater ille Johannes nomina magna
Cui Whethamstedi parvula villa dedit :
Triticeæ in tumulo signant quoque nomen aristæ,
Vitam res claræ non monumenta notant."

On each side of the monuments is the inscription, "Valles habundabunt," and the abbot's arms—three ears of wheat. Mr. Ridgway Lloyd concludes, from a passage in the records of the monastery, that it is the chantry, not of Abbot Wheathamstead, but of Abbot Wallingford (1476—1484). The shields charged with wheat ears afford, he contends, no proof to the contrary, as they are also found on the altar-screen, which was known to have been erected by William Wallingford, and the Latin inscription, which is in late seventeenth-century characters, only shows that it was at that time supposed to be the tomb of Abbot Wheathamstead, designed and executed in his lifetime. Sir Gilbert Scott has suggested that Abbot Wallingford may have placed the wheat-ears and motto on his own tomb out of veneration for the memory of his illustrious predecessor. In this tomb is placed one of the most beautiful brasses extant. It is the brass of an abbot in his pontifical robes, bearing this inscription in Lombardic characters—
"Hic jacet Dominus Thomas quondam Abbas hujus monasterii." The "Lord Thomas" was the Abbot de la

Mare, thirtieth abbot. It is believed to be of Flemish workmanship. The gravestones of four successive abbots may be seen at the foot of the altar-steps, and the one nearest to the tomb of Wheathamstead is supposed to be that of Abbot de la Mare. There are many monumental stones in the pavement of this part of the church, upon some of which are the remains of brass figures and inscriptions, which were mutilated by the Puritans. One of these is the brass figure of a knight in armour, a son of an Earl of Kent. Another brass is to the memory of a monk, supporting a heart between his hands, and a scroll with the legend from the 51st Psalm, 10th verse, "Cor mundum crea in me Deus." Near this brass is a stone containing an inscription issuing from the mouth of a monk, of which the following translation is given by the late Rev. Dr. Nicholson, in his valuable work on the Abbey Church, "Save, O Redeemer, thine ennobled workmanship, marked with the sacred light of thy countenance. Suffer not those for whom thou hast paid the penalty of death to be destroyed through the deceit of devils." Another brass is to the memory of Richard Stondon, a priest of the Abbey. Near the north door is a stone which formerly contained the representation in brass, under a Gothic canopy, of Abbot Stoke. On a large stone on the left is the matrix of a brass containing the figure of a mitred abbot, holding the pastoral staff, and the following inscription—"Hic quidam terra tegitur, peccati solvens debitum, cui nomen non imponitur, in libro vitæ sit conscriptum," "One is here covered with earth, paying the debt of sin, whose name is not placed on this record. May it be written in the Book of Life." It has been conjectured that this is the memorial of Abbot John Moote (1396-1401). The brass of the lower part of the effigy is a palimpsest. All these monumental relics have been left undisturbed.

The massive pulpit in the north-east corner of the tower is the gift of the Freemasons of England. The work was executed by Mr. Miskin, of St. Albans, at a cost of about £650, from the designs of Mr. John O. Scott. The pulpit is of the Decorated order. It has a massive hexagonal base in one block of Derbyshire fossil marble, on which rest six strong quartette clustered shafts, with moulded clustered marble bases and caps supporting the floor, and a bold, deep moulded overhanging marble cornice, the plan of this being circular in form, with large segmental curves leading into, and stopped by, five smaller segments with terminals, forming the floor of the niches above. The body of the pulpit is worked in Tisbury stone, and is also circular in form, with five niches, having groined and decorated canopies springing from moulded caps supported by slender marble columns on moulded bases, the responds and cresting carved; the space between the niches has moulded mullions and transoms, forming six elaborate tracery panels, the four top panels having richly carved foliated centres, the two lower having shields with masonic emblems, and the arms, name, and number of the Lodge that subscribed for the figure adjoining. Three of these niches have figures—the one in the south-west niche, given by the Watford Lodge, being " David with the Harp " ; the centre niche, " Solomon holding the Temple," given by the Halsey (St. Albans) Lodge ; the north-east, " Zerrubbabel, with Plan of the Temple," given by the Gladsmuir (Barnet) Lodge. The remaining two niches are at present vacant. The figures were sculptured by Messrs. Farmer and Brindley, of London. There is also between the niches in front of the top panels a delicate out-work of tracery supported by the canopy columns. The pulpit steps are of solid marble. The gift derives peculiar appropriateness from the fact that the original church built by King Offa in the eighth century was erected by him and the " Hond Masons," to the memory of St. Alban, and that according to the Guild legends St. Alban himself was intimately associated with the Masons. In these he is claimed as the patron of Freemasons. The earliest mention of St. Alban in connection with masonry is to be found in the Prose Constitutions, among MSS. of the British Museum of date 1425. There we read :—

"And St. Alban loved well Masons, and he gave them first their charges and manners first in England, and he ordained convenient times to pay for the travail."

This tradition is repeated and amplified in numerous other Guild legends. In the Lansdowne MS., A.D. 1560, we find these words :—

"St. Alban was a worthy Knight and Steward of the King, his household, and had government of his realm, and also of the making of the walls of the said town, and he loved well masons, and cherished them much, and made their pay right good, for he gave them 3 and vid. a week and iiid.; before that time all the land a mason took but one penny a day and his meat, till St. Alban mended it, and he gave them a charter of the King and his 'Councell,' for to hold a general assembly, and gave it to name assembly."

In the Antiquity MS., of date 1686, is this further statement :—

"And he gott them a charter from the King and his 'Counsell,' to hold a general 'Counsell,' and gave itt to name 'Assemblie,' thereat he was himself, and did help to make Masons and gave them charges as you shall heare afterwards."

The Prince of Wales, the Grand Master of the Order, and the Duke of Albany were among the subscribers to the pulpit, which was presented and unveiled with due ceremony on the 16th of July, 1883, by the Provincial Grand Master of Hertfordshire, Brother T. F. Halsey, M.P. The sermon upon the occasion was preached by the Grand Chaplain of England, the Rev. W. Oswell Thompson, M.A., Vicar of Hemel Hempstead.

We now pass out of the presbytery into the north aisle, the architecture of which is Early English. Here we observe the handsome stone groined roof, with the sacred monogram, "I H C," the first three letters of the Greek form of the name of Jesus. The wall arcading of this aisle has been extensively repaired, many large fragments of it having been found buried in the aisle. An earlier doorway, which had been filled with rubble work, was also discovered. The inner arch of this doorway was found distributed in fragments about the abbey, and these fragments were repaired and restored to their original position. The Decorated window over the arch has also been restored. Proceeding into the north transept, we find that the extreme simplicity of the architecture in this part of the church proves that it is of early Norman date, the work, no doubt, of Abbot Paul, in the last quarter of the eleventh century, soon after the introduction of the Norman style into England. The remains of a curious fresco (probably of the fifteenth century), representing the unbelief of St. Thomas, may be seen on the east wall; and in the ceiling a representation of the martyrdom of St. Alban has been carefully restored. Two apsidal chapels, which formerly stood on the east side of the north and south transepts, were removed in the fifteenth century, when windows were placed in the arches, and altars in the recesses. The remains of one of the altars are still to be seen. The large windows at the end of the transepts are altogether of a different style and period from the architecture surrounding them. The window in the north transept replaced that erected by William de Trumpington in the thirteenth century. The southern window was placed there about the year 1703, the former window having been destroyed by the wind in a storm. In the south transept two blocked windows of Abbot Trumpington have been opened and restored. On each side of the transepts is a number of semi-circular arches with stone columns and large capitals. These arches are something like those in the interior of the tower, and they open into the passage which runs through the wall of the church. The north transept is the supposed site of the martyrdom of St. Alban. In this transept two Norman windows, which had been closed for centuries, and a north door, have been opened out, and in one of these windows a curious watch-chamber was discovered.

On the west side of the transept is the spiral staircase, by which we may ascend the tower, and on reaching its summit we are well rewarded for the toilsome ascent by the interesting view we obtain of the town and the extensive and beautiful panorama of the surrounding country. The tower contains a fine peal of eight bells, of which the tenor is said to weigh 25 cwt. The clock and chimes have been re-erected, and some additions have been made to them. After descending the tower we return into the presbytery, and thence into the south aisle.

CHAPTER XII.

South Aisle of the Presbytery—Discovery of Perpendicular Doorway and Screen—Altar-Table—Memorial Window—Monumental Inscriptions—Altar-Tomb—Tomb of Humphrey, Duke of Gloucester—Inscription to his Memory—Saint's Chapel—Remains of Duke Humphrey—Discovery of the Shrine of St. Alban—Watcher's Gallery—Discovery of an Altar—Ante-Chapel and Shrine of St. Amphibalus—Lady Chapel—Sir Gilbert Scott's Report—Completion of the Lady Chapel by Abbot Eversden—Its Windows, &c.—Curious Passage—Abbot Norton—Receptacle of his Heart—Restorations—List of Abbots of St. Albans.

THE removal of the fragments of the shrine of St. Alban, which were discovered in the south aisle of the presbytery, brought to light a beautiful Perpendicular doorway with carved spandrils, which had given access to an extra-mural chapel, believed to be the one erected by Abbot Wheathamstead during his lifetime, and afterwards employed as a chantry chapel for Humphrey, Duke of Gloucester. A Perpendicular screen, which had been inserted in the wall about the middle of the fifteenth century, was also found, and this screen no doubt separated the south aisle from the chapel. Eastward of this screen are the remains of another chapel, of late Perpendicular work, with rose ornaments and the words "*Domine Miserere,*" and it is conjectured that Abbot Wheathamstead was, on his death in 1464, buried in this chapel. The wall arcading in the aisle has been skilfully restored, and new carved capitals added.

In the aisle of the saint's chapel, nearly opposite the steps leading into the chapel, we find an oblong table of stone, covered with a slab of dark marble, and marked with five small crosses. This has been supposed by some to be the original altar-table, which was removed from the choir after the suppression of the monastery. The painted glass window on the south side of the aisle is in memory of Dr. Watson, who died in 1839, and who was archdeacon of

St. Albans for twenty-three years. The subject of it is St. Alban on his way to execution. On the north side of the aisle are some quaint poetical inscriptions, to the memory of members of the Maynard family, some of whom represented St. Albans in Parliament in the reigns of Mary and Elizabeth. There is an altar-tomb between the tomb of Abbot Wheathamstead and the door of the saint's chapel. Our attention is now drawn to the magnificent tomb of

ALTAR-TOMB.

Humphrey, Duke of Gloucester. As we give an engraving of the tomb we forbear to enter into a minute description of it. By some the monument is attributed to Abbot Stoke, by others to Abbot Wheathamstead. However this may be, the tomb bears on it the arms of Wheathamstead and the wheat ears with which he always distinguished his works. The roof of the canopy is richly sculptured, and in the arches are ten shields of the duke's arms, with those of France and England in a border. There are a number of beautiful niches in the upper compartment of the tomb, and rich open work with arches in relief. The seventeen figures in the niches on the south side are supposed by Sandford, in his Genealogical History, to be the duke's royal ancestors; but most probably they were intended to represent the Kings of Mercia. One of them bears in his hand the model of a church, and this was no doubt meant to indicate King Offa as the founder of St. Albans Abbey. The iron grating is thought by some to be older than the monument itself, and is supposed to have been erected to give pilgrims and worshippers a sight of the shrine of St. Alban.

There was a Latin inscription to the memory of the "Good Duke Humphrey," on the east wall (now removed) of the aisle, written by a master of the Grammar School in the 17th century. It contained an allusion* to a religious fraud, practised by a man who pretended he had been miraculously restored to sight at the shrine of St. Alban, and said to have been exposed by Duke Humphrey. Shakespeare describes the legend in the second part of *Henry the Sixth*, act the second, the scene being laid at St. Albans—" Enter a townsman of St. Albans, crying ' A miracle! ' " The duke was also said to have " builded the Divinitie Schole at Oxford, which is a rare piece of work," and allusion is made to this fact in the inscription.

We now enter the saint's chapel, and here obtain a view of the north side of the monument to Duke Humphrey, as may be seen in the engraving. In the vault beneath are the remains of the good duke, which were accidentally discovered early in the last century. The body had been embalmed, and was found enclosed in a leaden coffin in an apparently perfect state of preservation. At the foot of the coffin is a representation of the crucifixion, painted on the wall, and a hand extended with a scroll, in which is written the legend " Blessed Lord, haue mercye on mee."

In the centre of the saint's chapel is the shrine of St. Alban, replaced on the spot where it stood for centuries—

* Fraudis ineptæ Detector.

an object of the most devout veneration. In the pavement are six grooves, which mark the place where the pillars of the shrine rested.

In several places round where the shrine stood the pave-

TOMB OF HUMPHREY, DUKE OF GLOUCESTER.

ment is worn into hollows. These indentations, it is said, are the result of the friction caused by the kneeling of successive generations of pilgrim worshippers at the shrine of the saint.

The most interesting and important discovery of the shrine of St. Alban—or, more properly speaking, of the pedestal of the shrine, which was shattered into fragments at the Reformation, and built into the walls then erected to cut off the lady chapel from the church—was made in 1872. About thirty years ago Dr. Nicholson discovered some pieces of the marble substructure of the shrine while opening out one of the walled-up arches at the east end of the saint's chapel. Nothing more, however, was found until February, 1872, when the workmen engaged in the restoration, whilst removing the materials which blocked up a doorway and screen in the wall of the south aisle of the presbytery, and subsequently the arches in the saint's chapel and presbytery aisle, discovered upwards of two thousand fragments of the shrine of St. Alban, besides portions of the shrine of St. Amphibalus. These fragments were, with marvellous skill and ingenuity, put together by Mr. Chapple, the clerk of the works, with the assistance of the foreman and two masons; and the re-constructed pedestal was set up on its original site in the saint's chapel. The structure not only possesses very great value from an antiquarian point of view, but also as a work of art. It was erected in the time of Abbot John de Marynes (1302-8), and is therefore of the Early Decorated period. The shrine bears some resemblance in form to that of Edward the Confessor in Westminster Abbey. It is composed entirely of Purbeck marble, with the exception of the canopy roofs, which are of clunch. Its height is eight feet three inches; its width three feet two inches; and its length eight feet seven inches. There are four canopied niches on each side, and two narrow ones at each end, with crocketed pediments, terminating in a highly-wrought cornice with cresting, and roofs of clunch, carved with reticulated tracery. These niches are not open to the ground, in order to form kneeling-recesses, as is the case with most shrines, but are closed by panels of elaborate tracery, with a quatrefoil in each panel. It is probable that the niches were intended for the reception of relics and offerings. The spaces between them have devices in gilding, on red and blue grounds; on some of them the three lions passant guardant of England and the fleur-de-lis of France, and stars and dots on the others. There are two apertures in the quatrefoils, which, it has been suggested, were made for the purpose of enabling diseased limbs, or the cloths to be applied to them, to be placed as near as possible to the martyr's remains. In the pediment at the west end is a sculptured representation of the decapitation of St. Alban, and near it are two angels swinging censers. In the corresponding pediment at the east end are figures representing the scourging of St. Amphibalus. In the tympanum below is a king, holding the model of a church. No doubt it is intended for King Offa, the founder of the Abbey. At each end on the south side is an angel swinging a censer, and pediments over the niches are filled with foliage of various kinds, including the vine, the maple, and the oak, with the double acorn. Between the pediments are two figures (there were formerly three) of kings, one of whom is supposed to be Offa, and the other St. Oswin, King of Mercia. On the north side, which is very imperfect, there is a seated figure of a bishop or abbot, which Mr. Ridgway Lloyd conjectures may represent St. Wolstan, Bishop of Worcester, who died in 1095. The cornice is richly sculptured with maple, whitethorn, and other leaves. Three twisted pillars on each side of the shrine appear to have stood detached, and may have borne the tapers which were lighted on festival days. Upon the pedestal rested the feretrum, or shrine proper, containing the saint's relics, which was no doubt destroyed for the sake of the precious metals and jewels of which it was composed.*

On the north side of the saint's chapel is the watcher's gallery, of oak, with quaint carvings on the frieze. In this gallery a monk was stationed, called the Custos Feretri. Here the monks kept silent watch day and night over the rich shrine of St. Alban, and the offerings which were placed on it by the pilgrims who came to pray for the help and intercession of the saint. The remains of an altar were discovered some years ago in the east wall of the chapel, and, protected

* For these details we are considerably indebted to Mr. Ridgway Lloyd's "Architectural and Historical Account of the Shrines of St. Alban and St. Amphibalus."

by glass, we find the figure in distemper of an archbishop, probably an Archbishop of York in the twelfth century.

We have now to visit the ante-chapel, and chapel of the Virgin, at the extreme eastern end of the Abbey, which since the Reformation had been separated from the main body of the church by a public passage, and blocked up arches. As we have before mentioned, the passage has, during the restoration, been diverted, and the arches have been re-opened. On arriving at the ante-chapel we find that it contains the pedestal of the shrine of St. Amphibalus, fragments of which were also discovered in 1872. This pedestal, however, is in a much more imperfect state than that of the shrine of St. Alban. The fragments are of finely-carved white stone, or clunch, and the north and south faces bear the initials of Ralph Witechurch, sacrist of the Abbey in the time of Abbot de la Mare (1349—1396). The nobles who were slain after the battle of St. Albans were buried in this chapel. The new arcading of the ante-chapel is the gift of Lady Beckett, Mr. Henry Hucks Gibbs, and the Bishop of St. Albans. We now pass into the lady chapel. As we have already stated, the restoration of these chapels, which had been allowed to fall into a lamentable state of ruin and decay, has been undertaken, by means of a separate fund subscribed by the ladies of Hertfordshire, but at the time of writing operations have, we are sorry to say, been suspended owing to the exhaustion of the fund. In a report upon the lady chapel which Sir Gilbert Scott presented to the Marchioness of Salisbury, he says that this group of eastern chapels, as finished by Abbot Eversden between 1308 and 1326, offers as exquisite examples as it is possible to find of the two great phases of English modern-pointed architecture. The actual date of the chapels and of the eastern end of the church has never been precisely ascertained, though they could not have been begun before the year 1257. Matthew Paris records that in that year Abbot John de Hertford began to rebuild the eastern end of the church. No further mention is made, however, of this work by Matthew Paris or his successors. Before the re-construction, a great Norman apse formed the eastern boundary of the church. Sir Gilbert Scott was inclined to attribute the earlier portions of the work to the time of Abbot Norton (1260—1291). On the accession of Abbot Eversden in 1308, he completed the lady chapel, which had only been carried up as high as the string course beneath the windows; and he is also recorded to have covered in the space between the lady chapel and the presbytery. The style of Hugh Eversden is a phase of the Decorated Period quite distinct from that of the first architect. The side windows of the lady chapel, in which we see the work of Eversden, are very elaborate and beautiful examples of the later Decorated style. The mullions and jambs are enriched with a number of little carved figures or statuettes, and the ornaments are peculiarly characteristic of fourteenth century work. The eastern window Sir Gilbert Scott described as a singular combination of tracery with tabernacle work; and the easternmost bay on the south side " has an exquisite window above, consisting of a richly-traceried circle, placed within a curvilinear triangle, beneath which is a splendid range of niches, and beneath them again a gorgeous range of sedilia and piscinæ." The groining of the south isle of the antechapel contains some fine specimens of painting dating from the end of the thirteenth century. It is somewhat remarkable that the wall arcading on the south side of the chapels has cinquefoiled heads, while that on the north is trefoiled throughout. There are the remains of a very curious passage leading into the lady chapel from the altar in the south aisle dedicated to St. Mary of the Four Tapers. The passage was probably constructed to form a ready communication between this altar and the great altar at the east end of the lady chapel. A very elaborate open oak screen, portions of which still remain, once divided the ante-chapel from the lady chapel, and will no doubt be restored. While the workmen were lowering the floor of the south transept they discovered a cylindrical hole sunk in a block of stone, in which was found the lid of a small wooden box, of about five inches diameter, of Oriental design, and richly painted. Some Arabic characters are distinguishable on the lid of the box. It is supposed that it may have contained the heart of some person whose body was buried elsewhere. A theory that it was the receptacle for the heart of Abbot Norton, who was buried before the high altar is, says Mr. Ridgway Lloyd, founded on a mistranslation of a passage relating to him.

The roofs and ceilings of the lady chapel and ante-chapel have undergone very extensive repairs and restorations, and the ceiling of the north aisle of the ante-chapel has been newly groined, with carved bosses at the intersection of the ribs. The windows, which were very greatly mutilated and decayed, have now been restored to their original beauty—three by the general funds of the ladies' committee, and seven at the expense of individual ladies. Two new stained windows are the gifts of the Corporation and Livery Companies of the City of London, and another window is the gift of Mrs. Leigh, of Luton Hoo. The beautiful arcading (only a few fragments of which remained) and all the internal stone work have been restored in strict accordance with their ancient character. Money is, however, still needed to complete the restoration of this part of the Abbey, our description of which we can hardly conclude in a better way than by again quoting the words of Sir Gilbert Scott :—

"I can hardly imagine a moment of greater joy and thankful gratulation than that in which the chapels—restored so far as may be to their pristine beauty—are once again united with the parent church, and when the glorious series of scenes opening out one after another as you proceed from the western entrance—the nave, the choir, the sanctuary, the saint's chapel, with the beautiful shrine of the protomartyr, shall not, as now, stop at that point, but shall continue through the five arches, so long walled up, into the ante-chapel, with the shrine of St. Amphibalus in its midst, and on again through the open screen into the exquisite lady chapel."

We have now performed our pleasant office of cicerone to our visitor in his inspection of the grand old Abbey of St. Albans. There are many objects of interest in the church of which we have given but a very imperfect description, and others which we have been obliged to pass over altogether. We trust, however, that what has been said has sufficed to awaken the curiosity of the reader, and to lead him to investigate for himself what must so well repay the trouble of investigation.

The monastic buildings connected with the Abbey were all situated on the south and south-west sides of the church. Of these only the Great Gate House (west of the Abbey) remains. This venerable building is about one hundred and fifty feet distant from the church. It originally formed a grand entrance to the Abbey court, and was used by the abbots of St. Albans as a place for the incarceration of criminals. The large arch of entrance is obtusely pointed, and has a groined roof. The extent of the Abbey courtyard may still be traced in the remains of walls that surrounded it. The building was used as the gaol for the Liberty of St. Alban until the erection of the present gaol. It was afterwards converted into a school-house for the use of King Edward the Sixth's Grammar School, which for three centuries had had its home in the lady chapel. The chapter-house stood in front of the south transept, and the refectories, the great dormitory, and other buildings were ranged parallel with the nave.

We are now forced by the inexorable limits of our space to bring our task to a conclusion. The materials to our hand have been so abundant that we have felt the perplexity of an *embarras de richesses*. So ample are they that we might easily have extended this work to three or four times its present size. Enough has been said, however, to prove that the ancient city of St. Albans possesses most interesting memorials of the silent Past.

St. Albans :—Printed by Gibbs & Bamforth, Market Place.

ABBOTS OF ST. ALBANS.

		Began to Rule.			Began to Rule.
1.	Willegod	—	22.	William de Trumpington	1214
2.	Eadric	—	23.	John de Hertford	1235
3.	Vulsig	—	24.	Roger de Norton	1260
4.	Vulnoth	—	25.	John de Berkhamsted	1291
5.	Aedfrid	—	26.	John de Marynes	1302
6.	Ulsinus	—	27.	Hugh de Eversden	1308
7.	Aelfric	—	28.	Richard de Wallingford	1326
8.	Ealdred	—	29.	Michael de Mentmore	1335
9.	Eadmer	—	30.	Thomas de la Mare	1349
10.	Leofric	—	31.	John Moote	1396
11.	Aelfric 2nd	—	32.	William Heyworth	1401
12.	Leofstan	—	33.	John Wheathamstead	1420
13.	Frederic	1066	34.	John Stoke	1440
14.	Paul de Caen (First Norman Abbot)	1077		Wheathamstead re-elected	1451
15.	Richard de Albini	1097	35.	William Alban	1464
16.	Geoffery de Gorham	1119	36.	William Wallingford	1476
17.	Ralph de Gobion	1146	37.	Thomas Ramryge	1492
18.	Robert de Gorham	1151	38.	Thomas Wolsey	1521
19.	Symon	1167	39.	Robert Catton	1530
20.	Warren de Cambridge	1183	40.	Richard Boreman de Stevenache	1538
21.	John de Cella	1195			

www.ingramcontent.com/pod-product-compliance
Lightning Source LLC
Chambersburg PA
CBHW020933180426
43192CB00036B/1034